IMAGES
of America

PASADENA'S
BUNGALOW HEAVEN

This classic 1910 Craftsman at 946 North Michigan Avenue in the heart of Bungalow Heaven was one of 12 on this block contractor Edward R. Zube built between 1909 and 1911. Although one of a kind, it incorporates typical Arts and Crafts elements: one story, front-facing porch, overhanging eves, wood shingle siding, with foundation, chimney, and elephantine porch piers and walls of native Arroyo stone. (Photograph by James Staub.)

ON THE COVER: The "Japo-Swiss" bungalow at 815 North Mentor Avenue, the district's western boundary, was built for $3,200 in 1912. It was made for James and Ella Falconer, retirees from Minneapolis, by the design-build firm of Kieft and Hetherington. One of seven homes the firm built in the neighborhood, it was featured in the 2009 Bungalow Heaven 20th anniversary Home Tour after extensive renovation. (Photograph by James Staub.)

IMAGES
of America

PASADENA'S
BUNGALOW HEAVEN

Julianna Delgado and John G. Ripley

ARCADIA
PUBLISHING

Published by Arcadia Publishing
Charleston, South Carolina

Printed in the United States of America

Library of Congress Control Number: 2011935876

For all general information, please contact Arcadia Publishing:
Telephone 843-853-2070
Fax 843-853-0044
E-mail sales@arcadiapublishing.com
For customer service and orders:
Toll-Free 1-888-313-2665

Visit us on the Internet at www.arcadiapublishing.com

In 2009, neighbors gathered to install new street signs to honor Bungalow Heaven's 20th anniversary and listing in the National Register of Historic Places. Economist Bob Kneisel (center and in hat) was a resident since 1983 and championed the original landmark-district petition drive. This book is dedicated to all the residents, property owners, and supporters who continue to make Bungalow Heaven a great place to live. (Photograph by James Staub.)

CONTENTS

ACKNOWLEDGMENTS

This book is dedicated to those trailblazing visionaries who stood their ground and defeated the bulldozers in the 1980s, launching Bungalow Heaven as the model for landmark districts. Countless local volunteers have inspired others nationwide to protect historical resources for future generations. Through their practice, they have also brought urban conservation efforts to the forefront of environmental sustainability. Given space limitations and the series' emphasis, this volume features archival images, showing only a fraction of the remarkable homes restored through personal commitment and hard work. We hope it tempts the reader to come see them all firsthand.

Our work was made possible in part by the California Center for Land and Water Stewardship at California State Polytechnic University, Pomona, with assistance from the California Landscape Architectural Student Scholarship (CLASS) Fund. These friends helped with research and images: Catherine and Christopher Adde, Ronald Alcorn, Jane Apostol, Dennis Bedford, Jim Crandall, Glen Dawson, Juan de la Cruz, John DePew and Deborah Shepler, Linda Euler, Sidney Gally, Mary Gandsey, Terry Hartley and James Staub, Russell Hobbs, Jason Kastner, Bob Kneisel, Dr. Denise Lawrence, Dr. Kathleen Menzie Lesko, Gregory McReynolds, Kennon Miedema, Tina Miller, Eunice and Joaquin Montalvan, Richard Quirk, Tom Perkins, Martin Ratliff and Carol Polanskey, Tom and Cindy Rice, Ann Scheid, Karen Sugars, Leslie Tamppari and Wes Hsu, Melissa Townsend, Dale Trader, Bill and Karen Walter, and John and Kathy Wright.

We are also indebted to the American Institute of Architects, Pasadena and Foothill Chapter (John Luttrell, Jill Nicholson), Bungalow Heaven Neighborhood Association, California History Section of the California State Library (Kathleen Correia), City of Pasadena (Vince Bertoni, Jeff Cronin, Kevin Johnson, Vicrim Chima, Julia Garzon, and Loren Pluth), Huntington Library (Erin Chase, Alan Jutzi, Bill Frank, Susan Oatey, Anita Weaver, and Manuel Flores), Pasadena Museum of History (Laura Verlaque and Anuja Navare), Pasadena Public Library (Dan McLaughlin and Laurie Whitcomb), *Pasadena Star News* (Janette Williams), and Arcadia Publishing, especially Jerry Roberts and Donna Libert, our editors.

Our most heartfelt gratitude goes to our families and loving spouses, David Delgado and Donna Ripley, who inspire everything worthwhile that we do.

KEY TO IMAGE CREDITS. Unless otherwise indicated, the images appear courtesy of the following sources: photography by Frederick W. Martin and courtesy of the California History Room at California State Library in Sacramento, California (CSL); Collection of Juan de la Cruz (JdlC); Huntington Library in San Marino, California (HL); Pasadena Museum of History (PMH); photography by Flag Studio (FS-PMH); photography by J. Allen Hawkins (JAH-PMH); and Pasadena Public Library (PPL).

INTRODUCTION

"While the delight of bungalow life in California is largely attributable to the quality of climate," wrote Charles Francis Saunders in his 1913 book, *Under the Sky in California*, "a generous share of credit is due also to good architects and first-class builders who have brought into the country the best ideas of their art and craft." Saunders was a naturalist, photographer, and tenderfoot from Philadelphia who settled in northeast Pasadena. His home is now a landmark adjacent to Bungalow Heaven, the city's oldest and largest locally designated historic district. It includes about 1,100 bungalows in a mile-square area around McDonald Park. Once a prairie below the foothills, it was transformed by the end of the 1920s into a middle-class neighborhood containing the nation's finest collection of what Saunders called "delectable little dwellings, hardly any two just alike" of the American Arts and Crafts period. The neighborhood's appeal has endured.

As a new neighborhood in a developing region, Bungalow Heaven was fertile ground for experiments in domestic architecture. Modern, progressive thinking, from Frank Lloyd Wright, Charles and Henry Greene, Gustav Stickley and others, would influence popular designs to serve changing lifestyles and turn a profit. The bungalows built around the turn of the century would signify collectively a paradigm shift from the rigid formalism of the elitist Victorians, based on a class system, hereditary privilege, and prescribed gender roles, to British publisher William Morris's enlightened emphasis on elevating all forms of labor of the Industrial Revolution. Morris also emphasized marrying the "beautiful and functional" (that is, the "High Arts" with prosaic crafts), especially in homes for a growing, deserving, and democratic middle class.

In contrast to their Victorian-style predecessors, these new, modest, and yet uncorseted Arts and Crafts dwellings averaged about 1,200 square feet and one to one and a half stories. With restrained ornamentation and a nod to nature through the use of local materials, especially raw stone and wood, they were built on ample, 50-foot-wide lots that were relatively long and narrow. They were equipped with welcoming porches, open-flowing floor plans, built-in furniture, and plenty of operable windows to bring in light and air. They were simple, efficient, inexpensive, cheerful, leisurely, and comfortable. No product was better suited to take advantage of the valley nestled below the glorious San Gabriels. The bungalow brought the outside in, eliminated the need for servants, gave women free time from household drudgery, and provided for healthy outdoor living, sleeping, and recreating, becoming a haven from the impersonal workplace or ideal space for happy retirement. It is no wonder American bungalows first proliferated in California and why interest bloomed in restoring them at the turn of the millennium after a generation had grown up in the "Land of Sunshine's" cookie-cutter, suburban tract homes.

Bungalow Heaven's story begins long before its bungalows. It started before Saunders arrived from Pennsylvania and even before the Indiana colonists came, who sought refuge from a terrible winter and settled on the warm, fertile land near the Arroyo Seco. They settled in a place they called Pasadena, a Chippewa phrase interpreted popularly as "Crown of the Valley." The story begins in the 1860s with James Craig, an Irish engineer trained in waterworks. From a wealthy

Belfast line of linen merchants, Craig had already traveled the world when his steamer arrived in San Francisco. With backing from his family and friends, including Alexander Grogan, one of the city's influential founders, he headed south to improve his health and dabble in real estate. In 1869, Craig purchased 5,000 acres from local pioneers Hon. Benjamin D. Wilson and Dr. John S. Griffin of the old San Gabriel Mission land that had become Rancho San Pasqual. In the eastern end of the valley, the Craig Tract, later renamed Grogan when the loans were settled, included Craig's homestead, called "The Hermitage." The rest of his arid property, suitable at first only for grazing, was soon subdivided, sold off, and transformed into lush vineyards and citrus groves with water that flowed down from the mountains into an efficient irrigation system.

By 1886, the year the city of Pasadena due west of Craig's property incorporated, a transplanted New Yorker and one of the city's enterprising pioneers, Romayne "Barney" Williams, owned its central gathering place, Williams Hall. To make his fortune in the real estate boom of the late 1800s, Williams sold off his nearby homestead, the land that is now Central Park, and purchased 80 acres in the Grogan Tract far from the city's bustling downtown. His Queen Anne mansion built by friend and local architect Harry Ridgeway near the corner of Hill Avenue and Mountain Street, aptly named "Hillmont," still struts at the eastern edge of Bungalow Heaven as a reminder of Victorian-era splendor.

When the boom burst, Williams lost his fortune, eventually leaving Pasadena forever. Nonetheless, with the coming of the San Gabriel Valley Railroad that linked Pasadena to Los Angeles and the burgeoning tourism trade, the city continued to grow outward. By 1906, a streetcar system running north and south along Lake Avenue, one of Pasadena's main arterials and Bungalow Heaven's western boundary, enabled development in the northeast, and the area was officially annexed. From the late 1800s until World War I, Jennie Keil built her home on Mentor Avenue, C.C. Thompson subdivided his 80-acre apricot orchard, and J.H. Woodworth and Son and other real estate firms carved up the remaining Grogan Tract. The once rural area mushroomed with Craftsman-style bungalows built typically by contractors, about half on speculation. After World War I, when a flood of new residents came into Southern California, the neighborhood was soon dotted with popular Colonial Revival–style homes. Larger ones towards the eastern end, on Chester and Holliston Avenues near Williams's Hillmont, reflected the later appreciation for other revival styles, especially Tudor and Spanish Colonial. By the Great Depression, the area had been completely subdivided into small lots and almost fully developed, having grown eastward seven blocks from Lake to Hill Avenues.

After World War II, ranch-style homes came into vogue in massive, automobile-oriented tracts. Growth sprawled out farther from city centers, leaving older, more compact neighborhoods to deteriorate. In the mid-1980s, however, a grassroots movement sprang from the bypassed Bungalow Heaven area. It took flattening a 1911 Craftsman bungalow and replacing it with an ugly apartment building for residents to pound on doors until they gathered 55 percent of the property owners' signatures, enough to halt demolitions, reduce densities, and gain protections. In November 1989, in response to the petition drive, the city council declared this as "Bungalow Heaven," Pasadena's first local landmark district and a model for 17 more to follow, spearheading a preservation campaign that revitalized the entire city. A major article in the *Los Angeles Times* on February 9, 1990, showcased the new district designed to "protect the character of 900 bungalows," describing the appeal to young couples as an "attractive alternative to a tract." By 2002, with widespread interest in single-family homes with character built to human scale on walkable streets, *Sunset Magazine* named Bungalow Heaven among the "West's Best" neighborhoods. Property values soared. *Cottage Living* ranked it among the nation's "Top Ten" neighborhoods. On April 10, 2008, following the city's nomination, the Bungalow Heaven Historic District was listed in the State and National Registers. The next year, the 20th anniversary of the district's founding, the American Planning Association deemed it a "Great Neighborhood" for its commitment to civic engagement and lovingly restored reminder of a simpler, healthier way of life. In 1913, booster Charles Francis Saunders wrote, "One of the hard-worked words in California of recent years is bungalow." The same is true a century later.

One

BEFORE THE BUNGALOWS

During the California mission period, Rancho San Pasqual lands—like this spot near the Arroyo Seco, a tributary of the Los Angeles River—were used mainly for raising livestock. In the 1870s, Midwesterners came for the mild winters, water supply, and fertile soil and formed the San Gabriel Orange Growers Association, naming this place Pasadena, a Chippewa phrase meaning "the valley." (PMH A5-14.)

Around 1863, Benjamin Davis "Don Benito" Wilson (left) from Tennessee, Los Angeles's second mayor and a three-term California state senator, and Dr. John Strother Griffin (right) from Virginia, chief army medical officer, acquired for $1,800 the 13,500-acre Rancho San Pasqual granted to Manuel Garfias. Their land sale launched Pasadena's development. Mount Wilson looms over the San Gabriel Valley, and Wilson Avenue crosses through Bungalow Heaven. (PMH People-W; G.)

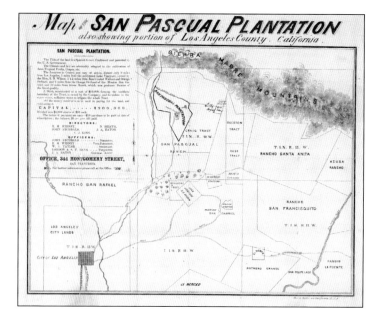

This 1870 map shows Rancho San Pasqual tracts. Bungalow Heaven is within the 5,000 acres James Craig purchased from Don Benito Wilson and John Griffin on May 10, 1869, for $31,250, which was loaned by family and friends William and Alexander Grogan, a San Francisco pioneer. The tract name changed from Craig to Grogan when the loans came due. It was surveyed for subdivision in 1876 and entirely under cultivation by 1894. (HL.)

Craig, an Irish hydrological engineer, obtained water rights and bored the first artesian well. His adobe on his 143-acre ranch in the Grogan Tract, "The Hermitage," is the oldest standing house in Pasadena. By 1899, Craig had become a citrus authority and managed the Precipice Canyon Water Company incorporated in 1887 but died in a tunneling accident in Eaton Canyon (shown here). (Photograph by Lucius Jarvis, PMH C2-1-8.)

In 1865, Harvard-educated Judge Benjamin S. Eaton acquired from Eliza Griffin Johnston the 260-acre Fair Oaks Ranch, located west of his namesake falls and canyon. An irrigation expert, he planted 35,000 grapevines and helped broker the $25,000 land sale from his brother-in-law John Griffin and Don Benito Wilson to the California Colony of Indiana that founded Pasadena. Railroad developer James Fillmore Crank bought Fair Oaks in 1876. (JAH-PMH H11-7B.)

Don Benito Wilson (1811–1878) came to California in 1841 and purchased the 128-acre Rancho Huerta de Cuati (now the City of San Marino) in 1854 from Hugo Reid's widow. He renamed the ranch Lake Vineyard and raised his family (his grandson Gen. George S. Patton was born there in 1885) along with grapes and oranges, shipping over a million from 16,500 trees in 1874. (PMH A2-15-4.)

Bavarian immigrant Leonard J. Rose (second from right), a future state senator, bought 2,000 acres of Rancho Santa Anita for citrus growing and viniculture. Called Sunny Slope, it became the largest winery in Southern California after the San Gabriel Valley Railroad that James Fillmore Crank championed began operating. Rose eventually subdivided the land, creating Lamanda Park, which he sold in 1887 to breed horses at his "Rose-Meade" ranch. (HL.)

Water from Eaton Canyon, originally called El Precipicio, flowed south to reservoirs on most of the ranches east of Pasadena for farming. In his 1886 address at the Irrigation Convention in San Francisco, James DeBarth Shorb (Wilson's son-in-law, agent, and Los Angeles County treasurer) declared, "The magnificent results . . . to follow the bringing of land and water together" and "usefully appropriating waters which have been running wastefully to the sea." (PPL.)

While the western end of the valley grew into the cities of Pasadena and South Pasadena, the eastern remained rural long after. It became a premier wine and citrus-producing region once the railroad came. This 1,100-acre property, among the last annexed into Pasadena, was the vineyard Charles Houston Hastings inherited from his father. Called Hastings Ranch, it was subdivided after 1942 and developed into large, suburban housing tracts. (PPL.)

The estate of renowned American artist William F. Cogswell opened in 1877 as the Sierra Madre Villa Hotel, the area's first grand resort. On 500 acres northeast of Pasadena, it catered to visitors and health-seekers, becoming an attraction that launched tourism as an economic base. Don Benito Wilson renamed the county road (along Pasadena's original northern boundary) Villa Street, expecting it to link the town to the hotel. (PMH H84-1c.)

Many place and street names—including Allen, Brigden, Craig, Hastings, Kinneloa—originated from those of influential families that owned the eastern ranches, shown at Fox Ridges overlooking Eaton Canyon in this early 1900s Harold Parker group portrait. A great inventor, white-bearded Prof. Thaddeus Sobieski Coulincourt Lowe (second row, sixth from left), built the Mount Lowe Incline Railway, the world's first electric mountain system and a major tourist attraction. (HL.)

In 1878, when the Grogan Tract was subdivided, Englishman William R. Allen bought 474 acres and part of Eaton's Fair Oaks Ranch above what is now New York Drive in Altadena. He named it the Sphinx, having lived in Cairo, Egypt. Allen died in 1886, leaving a widow, nine children, and this mansion. It was torn down in 1928 to make way for a later subdivision. (PMH H5-32A.)

In 1880, after an asthma-curing stay at the Sierra Madre Villa Hotel, Abbott Kinney, the Maryland tobacco millionaire known for developing Venice, California, purchased 550 acres near Eaton Canyon and built his palatial home, Kinneloa. A conservationist and friend of John Muir, Kinney was the first chair of California's Board of Forestry and a US Indian commissioner alongside Helen Hunt Jackson. (Photograph by T.G. Norton, PMH K2-45a.)

In 1883, Charles James Fox II, a real estate developer and son of the British photographer, while living in a downtown Los Angeles mansion at Third and Olive Streets bought 108 acres from homesteader Carlos Cruz for $2,000, plus adjacent land from Allen and Kinney. In 1913, he retired to Rockwood (renamed Fox Ridges by daughter Mary Beatrice), the estate he built on a bluff overlooking Eaton Canyon. (HL.)

Mary Beatrice Fox (on the bridge, second from left, next to the boy) is shown during this 1918 outing in Eaton Canyon. A lifelong friend of architect Julia Morgan, her classmate at the University of California, she would later inherit Fox Ridges and sell the canyon portion of the property in 1950 to Los Angeles County as part of the 190-acre Eaton Canyon Natural Area Park. (HL.)

Romayne "Barney" Williams, a dry goods clerk from New York, came in 1877, when Samuel Washburn bought Pasadena's first general store from postmaster Henry T. Hollingsworth, which had been built by his colonist father. Williams became manager and purchased the business in 1880, the year President Hayes visited. In 1883, he built this new store on the northeast corner of Fair Oaks Avenue and Colorado Street. (PMH B8-B25a.)

Williams Hall was the center of civic life. It housed a general merchandise store downstairs, with the first post office, telephone, and electric lights. Enlarged in 1885, the Williams Block (razed in 1902) had a meeting hall and stage upstairs that could seat 500 people for entertainment, business, worship, and politics. On May 13, 1886, Pasadena incorporated by a vote held upstairs in this building. (PPL.)

In 1886, five acres around Fair Oaks Avenue and Colorado Street were auctioned off to spark development. The First National Bank opened across from Williams Hall, both designed by local architect Hamilton "Harry" Ridgeway, who came from Canada in 1878. Builder Clinton Ripley and Ridgeway opened the first millworks, and along with Barney Williams they were the first three masters of Pasadena's Masonic Lodge No. 272. (Photograph by Ellis A. Bonine, PMH B2-3b.)

Barney Williams, who became a prominent citizen, arrived nearly penniless but soon purchased five acres on Fair Oaks Avenue. This 1883 photograph shows his homestead, present-day Central Park (Pasadena's first, acquired in 1902), with his wife, Ella, holding their son and only child Gilbert. Williams sold the land for $200,000 during the boom and purchased 80 acres "way out" in the Grogan Tract. (Photograph by T.G. Norton, PMH H45-3.)

In October 1887, Barney Williams completed this 4,329 square-foot, Ridgeway-designed Queen Anne jewel at the corner of North Hill Avenue and East Mountain Street, aptly named Hillmont. With a base faced with green Tehachapi sandstone and 32 stained-glass windows, it cost over $23,000. Five years later, Williams had lost his fortune, eventually moving to Los Angeles, where he died in 1909. (Photograph by Kevin Johnson, City of Pasadena.)

Around 1892, retired British colonel Adolphus De Gruchy Sutton acquired a 10-acre orange grove across from Barney Williams's Hillmont and built a homemade clay tennis court. In 1904, while at Pasadena High School, May Godfrey Sutton, the youngest of the colonel's four athletic daughters, won the US championships. The next year, she became the first American to win a singles title at Wimbledon. (Courtesy of the Library of Congress.)

BIRDS EYE VIEW OF PASA

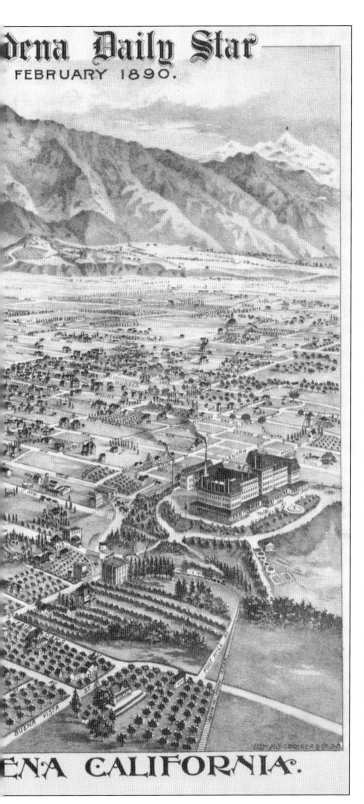

dena Daily Star

FEBRUARY 1890.

ENA CALIFORNIA.

In September 1885, the Los Angeles and San Gabriel Valley Railroad Company, with James Fillmore Crank as president, opened its line connecting the Pasadena area to intercontinental service via downtown Los Angeles, boosting agriculture and tourism and opening the floodgates for land speculation. In 1886–1887, there were 433 subdivision maps filed and over 400 homes built. Real estate sales at about $7 million in 1886 doubled the next year. The bubble burst in early 1888. From 1880 to 1890, the population grew from 390 to 10,000 residents. This remarkable, 1890 bird's-eye map was drawn from west of the costliest building, the Raymond Hotel, showing the results of the land boom. The unincorporated northeast is still ranch land. The two largest structures within the oval, indicating today's Bungalow Heaven, are Barney Williams's Hillmont and the Sutton mansion (no longer standing) across Mountain Street. (HL.)

21

Properties above Washington Boulevard, Bungalow Heaven's northern boundary, are shown here in the early 1900s. In 1883, orchardist Ezra Dane from Massachusetts purchased 160 acres west of James Fillmore Crank's Fair Oaks property. Two years later, the Danes built a Victorian ranch house, "Sunnyridge on the Highlands," that still stands at 1460 North Michigan Avenue. In 1912, they subdivided their land, which was annexed into Pasadena in 1925. (PMH H11-4c.)

Some Victorian houses built by early farmers on smallish plots, establishing the development pattern, remain in Bungalow Heaven. In 1885, Jennie Keil built the first at 714 North Mentor Avenue on 17 acres near Lake Avenue and Illinois Street (now East Orange Grove Boulevard). The 700-block of North Mentor (opened in 1886) was in the city limits, with the remainder annexed in 1904 with North Pasadena. (Photograph by James Staub.)

Bungalow Heaven's northernmost subdivision, Washington Square, was originally Charles C. Thompson's 80-acre apricot orchard, shown in this early-1900s photograph by Charles Francis Saunders. The valley's biggest producer of dried fruits, Thompson served on the Pasadena Lake Vineyard Land and Water Company Board. He also served as first president and manager of the 1893 Fruit Growers Association and vice president of the short-lived Highland Railway operating on Lake Avenue. (HL.)

Nature writer and amateur photographer Charles Francis Saunders (1859–1941) from Philadelphia moved into this bungalow at 580 North Lake Avenue in 1906. Named Ah-Tshi-Quah-Nah, it was restored in 2005 and is now a locally designated landmark. The year Saunders arrived, the city limits moved eastward to Hill Avenue with the East Pasadena annexation that incorporated the entire Bungalow Heaven area northeast of his property, including Thompson's apricot orchard. (HL.)

Charles Saunders and first wife, Elisabeth (died 1910), both avid gardeners, are seen having tea under their backyard arbor. They moved to the "Land of Sunshine" after their 1902 honeymoon trip to California to improve her health, collaborate on botanical publications, and enjoy outdoor life. In 1921, Saunders met second wife, Mira Barrett Culin, at the Pasadena Garden Club. The creek and lagoon in the background were later channelized. (HL.)

Charles Saunders, shown later in life sometime after 1929, became a noted author and collector of southwestern Native American artifacts who helped raise interest in restoring California's missions. He advocated living the simple "Life in a Bungalow" in his popular 1913 book *Under the Sky in California*, calling them "delectable little dwellings" and claiming, "one of the greatest attractions of California Bungalow life is its freedom from conventionality." (HL.)

Two

THE DEVELOPERS

Catherine and Mary Helen Johnston pose in front of their home at 1191 Mar Vista Avenue around 1920. Starting about 1905, developers, small speculative builders, and individual families constructed bungalows that became the homes of hundreds of middle-class American families like the Johnstons. The Arts and Crafts (or Craftsman) movement guided the design of these efficient, comfortable, "artistic," and moderately priced homes. (Courtesy of Glen Dawson.)

A few small-scale developers built multiple bungalows in limited sections of the neighborhood, establishing their architectural flavor. One of these firms, the Coast Construction Company of Los Angeles, built a series of houses in the 700 and 800 blocks of North Michigan Avenue in 1907–1908. This one at 740 North Michigan was sold to Edward Off and later became the residence of local historian Fred Shoop. (FS-PMH 2-49-249.)

Like many of the 1907 Coast bungalows, 772 North Michigan Avenue featured the spiky, rustic stonework that led later to the nickname "the boulder bungalows." The construction cost for each 1907 Coast house was estimated at around $2,900; Coast's designers are unidentified. A number of very similar bungalows exist near Arlington Avenue and Venice Boulevard in Los Angeles. (FS-PMH 2-49-251.)

Another 1907 bungalow by Coast Construction was at 817 North Michigan Avenue. It was used as a rental by Coast until 1911, when traveling salesman Wilbur Shampine bought it. Coast's president was Ross W. Smith of Los Angeles, who in 1906 had been the partner of Arthur S. Heineman in the Heineman-Smith Construction Company; however, there is no evidence of Heineman involvement in Coast. (FS-PMH 2-49-253.)

The only Coast bungalow on the block that was built for a specific client was 723 North Michigan Avenue, which was commissioned by Harry Van Buskirk in 1908 for $2,000. Van Buskirk (1872–1952) was a Throop Institute (now the California Institute of Technology) mathematics professor. He and his wife, Nora, lived on Michigan Avenue until 1921. This photograph of the professor was probably taken on the Caltech campus about 1920. (PMH People-V.)

Coast's bungalow at 840 North Michigan Avenue is almost hidden by foliage in this 1914 photograph. The stone chimney on the right is barely visible. The operations manager for Coast Construction was William H. Smith of South Pasadena, son of wealthy railroad magnate Charles Warren Smith. William H. Smith does not seem to have been related to Ross W. Smith, Coast's president. (FS-PMH 2-49-254.)

This home at 860 North Michigan Avenue was built in 1907 and featured many of the details and design elements that appeared repeatedly in Coast bungalows, including the shingled exterior, distinctive stonework, flaring apron at the base of the walls, and "whale's mouth" cut-outs in the ends of the beams and rafters. Both photographs on this page show examples of period awnings. (FS-PMH 2-49-255.)

WHAT CAN BE ACCOMPLISHED WITH THE ROUGHEST RED-
WOOD "SHAKES," REDWOOD TIMBER AND SIMPLE MASONRY.

This view of Coast's 1907 bungalow at 884 North Michigan Avenue appeared in Gustav Stickley's *Craftsman* magazine in November 1910 in an article titled, "How the California Bungalow Illustrates the Right Use of Building Materials." The author was Pasadena resident Helen Lukens Gaut, who is discussed later in this chapter. (PPL.)

Builder and designer Guy Stanley Bliss (1878–1919) provided design and construction services for a series of 17 speculative bungalows on Michigan and Chester Avenues in 1909 and 1910. They were financed by Albert Mercer (1874–1943), a banker and real estate speculator. Bliss built a total of 65 houses in Pasadena between 1904 and 1911. He unfortunately died during the 1918–1919 influenza epidemic. (Courtesy of Linda Euler.)

The 1909 bungalow at 875 North Michigan Avenue was constructed by Guy Bliss for Albert Mercer at a cost of $2,500. It is difficult to see in this 1914 photograph, but the front door is positioned so that it appears to go through the chimney. Bliss lived here briefly around 1910. (FS-PMH 2-49-256.)

Guy Bliss holds his daughter Helen on the front steps of 875 North Michigan Avenue around 1910. It was not unusual for builders to live for a time in houses they had constructed. Perhaps, while awaiting a buyer, Albert Mercer permitted Bliss to live here as a partial payment for the house. (Courtesy of Linda Euler.)

Helen Bliss (1908–1979) sits on a tiny chair next to her Christmas tree and toys on the driveway of 875 North Michigan Avenue around 1910. Some of her descendants still live in the Pasadena area. There is a china drinking cup hanging from the windowsill above the water spigot behind her. (Courtesy of Linda Euler.)

The bungalow at 810 North Michigan Avenue was another of the Guy Bliss jobs for Albert Mercer. It was built in early 1910 for $2,500. This photograph dates from 1914. A different photograph, together with a floor plan, appeared in the July 1914 issue of the *Ladies Home Journal* and also in its 1916 plan book *Journal Bungalows*. (FS-PMH 2-49-252.)

This image of 857 North Michigan Avenue appeared in the *Journal Bungalows* plan book in 1916. It was built by Guy Bliss for partners Albert Mercer and Henry Meyer in late 1909 at a cost of $2,500. Hipped roofs were uncommon on Pasadena Craftsman bungalows, but Bliss built several similar houses. The roof gave this bungalow a hint of Prairie School flavor. (Ripley collection.)

This 1930s snapshot shows the Campbell family in their front yard at 873 North Chester Avenue. Their home, almost hidden by foliage, was originally constructed by Guy Bliss in early 1910 for Albert Mercer at a cost of $2,500. The Campbells bought it in 1917 from Wacil Mercer, Albert Mercer's ex-wife. (Courtesy of Melissa Townsend.)

This snapshot shows owner John Campbell (1864–1937) working in the backyard of 873 North Chester, probably during the 1920s. Campbell was both a chemist and a nurseryman, and his love of plants is apparent in this and the preceding photograph. John and his wife, Anna, came to Pasadena from New Jersey. (Courtesy of Melissa Townsend.)

The largest house built by Guy Bliss in Bungalow Heaven was this two-story Craftsman house at 897 North Holliston Avenue. It was built apparently on speculation by a partnership consisting of Bliss, real estate broker Walter W. Ogier, and civil engineer Louis A. Bartlett. Bliss lived here briefly around 1911. At $6,000, the cost of this house exceeded the typical range for the neighborhood. (FS-PMH 3-49-361.)

Tom and Jeanne Perkins pose in front of the inglenook of their newly purchased house at 897 North Holliston Avenue on their wedding day in 1952. Thomas Gardner Perkins, originally from Idaho and schooled in Pasadena, was a California Institute of Technology (Caltech) and Jet Propulsion Lab engineer and expert in nuclear magnetic resonance. He built museum cases and exhibits that Jeanne designed for the Huntington, Getty, and others. (Tom Perkins collection.)

Child star Jeanne Devereaux Perkins, who left St. Louis with her mother in 1926 for New York's vaudeville theater, became an international prima ballerina who danced for royalty and appeared on stage and in films. She retired at age 40, moved to Pasadena in 1952, and directed the Devereaux Ballet Arts School until 1964. An active lecturer, writer, and preservationist, she passed away in July 2011. (Jeanne Devereaux Perkins collection.)

James Hamilton Gaut developed 25 properties in Bungalow Heaven. His wife, Helen Lukens Gaut, was a prolific magazine writer and daughter of Theodore Parker Lukens (1848–1918), a two-term Pasadena mayor, conservationist, and friend of John Muir. From left to right around 1897 are (front row) Ralph and Charlotte Jones, Helen's children from her first marriage; (back row) Helen, Theodore Lukens, and Helen's mother, Charlotte Dyer Lukens. (HL.)

The Gaut speculative bungalows were constructed beginning in 1910 and ending in 1914, when James Gaut was killed in an automobile accident. The earliest Gaut bungalow for which an historical photograph has been found is 1027 (formerly 1035) North Michigan Avenue. It was built by contractor Oliver Clyde Williams at a cost of $2,200 for James, who was the owner of record for all the Gaut bungalows. (FS-PMH 2-49-263.)

Oliver Clyde Williams (1880–1951) constructed 1001 North Michigan Avenue in 1911 for James Gaut at a cost of $2,600. Williams was the contractor for the Gauts' own home at 392 Arroyo Drive, which he designed with Helen Gaut. Given this design credit and her frequent articles on architecture in national home-building magazines, it is possible that she contributed to the design of the Gaut speculative bungalows. (FS-PMH 2-49-261.)

With 955 North Michigan Avenue at the end of 1911, James Gaut (1878–1914) expanded his role to include being the contractor in addition to owner of record. This $2,400 bungalow was similar to 1027 but featured a larger porch. Gaut married Helen Lukens Jones in 1906 and for a short time partnered with her father in real estate, opening his own office in 1910. (FS-PMH 2-49-258.)

James Gaut was the owner and builder of this $2,000 bungalow at 725 Mar Vista Avenue in 1912. Gaut built this basic design a total of five times, all in 1912. The other instances were 881 North Chester Avenue, 489 North Michigan Avenue (outside Bungalow Heaven), 1070 North Michigan, and 1302 Mar Vista. Lighter colors for the exteriors of bungalows began to become popular in the early 1910s. (FS-PMH 2-49-223.)

James Gaut's bungalow at 1125 North Michigan Avenue cost $2,000 in 1912. In a 1910 article in the *Craftsman*, Helen Gaut wrote, "There is something very attractive about the use of silver grey or white on the roof of a house built of dark shingles." Many bungalows had low rooflines that took advantage of composition roll roofing, which was watertight even if flat. (FS-PMH 2-49-265.)

Brickwork was a prominent feature of 995 North Michigan Avenue, built by James Gaut in early 1913 for $2,000. Helen Gaut (1872–1955) did not continue her husband's building company after his death in 1914, and her writing for national magazines tapered off, ending by 1920. Besides architecture, she had written articles on interior decoration, gardening, and motor touring; she also wrote and published songs. (FS-PMH 2-49-260.)

James Gaut's 1110 North Michigan Avenue bungalow was probably designed by Pasadena architectural draftsman George Palmer Telling (1876–1957). This image appeared in Telling's *Select California Bungalows* in 1921 (with a fake background). Most of the Gaut bungalows after mid-1913 seem to have been by Telling. This one cost $1,900 and was described by Telling as "rather odd in design . . . but attractive." (PMH.)

Bungalow of Seven Rooms Which Cost Approximately $2,650 Complete and Ready for Occupancy

James Gaut's 1155 East Orange Grove Boulevard bungalow was built in late 1913 for $2,500. This photograph appeared in an article by designer George Telling in the February 1917 issue of *Bungalow Magazine*. Telling ran a Pasadena-based plan service, advertising nationally. He came to Pasadena from his native Michigan in 1902 and was initially a real estate agent and a bookkeeper, switching to house designing in 1914. (JdlC.)

James Gaut, whose right was amputated by a train in 1910, changes a tire during a motor outing. The Gauts were avid early motorists, and Helen wrote articles on automobile travel for national and local periodicals. She was the first woman to drive to the summit of Mount Wilson via the intimidating Toll Road. (Photograph by Helen Lukens Gaut, PMH HLG-185.)

This house at 1185 North Holliston Avenue and a twin at 1207 North Holliston were the last James Gaut bungalows constructed. They were built in late 1913 (O. Clyde Williams, contractor; $3,500) and early 1914 (Gaut, builder; $3,800), respectively. George Telling was probably the designer. The size and cost of these two houses reflected the upscale development of the eastern part of Bungalow Heaven (see chapter five). (FS-PMH 2-49-177.)

ON THE left is a most attractive little shingled home, which cost $2220 to build. The exterior finish is a warm gray with dark trim. Inside there are five large rooms, with bath, cellar and screen porch. A particularly attractive feature of the living-room is a big brick fireplace.
—Designed by Edward R. Zube.

An article by Helen Lukens Gaut in the July 1913 issue of *Ladies Home Journal* included this image of 1002 North Michigan Avenue, crediting the design to Edward R. Zube, who built it on speculation in 1909 for $1,900. Zube (1864–1947) developed a section of Michigan Avenue near James Gaut's houses, building 12 bungalows between 1909 and 1911. (PPL.)

Edward Zube built 915 North Michigan Avenue on speculation in 1911 at a cost of $2,500. He was a native of Germany who came to the United States in 1873 at the age of nine with his parents and sister. They settled in Connecticut, ending up by 1883 in Meriden, where Edward became a carpenter. He became a naturalized US citizen in 1888. (Photograph by Helen Lukens Gaut, PMH HLG-87.)

Owner Richard Stoneman converted 915 North Michigan Avenue into a two-story duplex in 1915. The addition was designed and built by the Rossiter-Banfield Company at a cost of $975. Harry Banfield started his own office in 1913 after working for the Foss Designing and Building Company (see chapter three). He started the Rossiter-Banfield design-build firm in 1914 with Arthur Rossiter. (Photograph by James Staub.)

The bungalow at 921 North Michigan Avenue was constructed by Edward Zube on speculation in late 1911 for $2,400. Zube moved to Pasadena from Connecticut in 1904 at the age of 40 and immediately went into business as a builder and contractor. He constructed about fifty houses before retiring in 1921, eighteen of them in Bungalow Heaven. (FS-PMH 2-49-257.)

Unfortunately, the site of this 1913 Zube bungalow at 1311 North Mentor Avenue became part of a parking lot behind the businesses on Washington Boulevard around 1955. It was built for William Streeter at a cost of $3,000. In the background is part of 1321 North Mentor, another 1913 Zube house that was removed to develop the parking lot. (FS-PMH 2-49-242.)

The City Builders Investment Company of Los Angeles developed portions of Mar Vista Avenue on speculation in 1912; its first three were 1286, 1278, and 1321 Mar Vista in the spring of 1912. This photograph shows 1286 Mar Vista in 1914. City Builders was both owner and builder, as it was with all of its houses here. This $1,700 bungalow was sold to Birdie Hodding. (FS-PMH 2-49-226.)

William and Etta Chapman bought 1278 Mar Vista Avenue, built by City Builders for $1,700. The large Los Angeles architectural firm of Norman F. Marsh (1871-1955) provided the designs for all eight of the City Builders houses. Marsh, a resident of South Pasadena, did a large volume of commercial and institutional work, including laying out Venice, California (noted for its canals), for Pasadenan Abbot Kinney in 1904. (FS-PMH 2-49-225.)

City Builders erected 1191 Mar Vista Avenue in the summer of 1912 for $2,400. It was bought by Frank Forbes and used as a rental. In the summer of 1917, it was bought by Charles and Isabelle Johnston and was their family home and sometimes office for the next 55 years. This family snapshot shows the house around 1920. (Courtesy of Glen Dawson.)

Mary Helen Johnston (1916–2002) waves the Stars and Stripes on the front lawn of 1191 Mar Vista Avenue (with 1199 Mar Vista in the background). She married Glen Dawson in 1940, and they built a home in the San Rafael area of Pasadena. During Glen's World War II Army service, Mary Helen moved back to her parents' house on Mar Vista with their young son Keith. (Courtesy of Glen Dawson.)

The Johnston family is sharing a meal in their dining room at 1191 Mar Vista Avenue in this early snapshot taken without a flash. The typical dark-stained woodwork can be seen. The hanging electric fixtures have wicker shades. Also visible are a treadle sewing machine to the left of the table and a Mission-style rocking chair in the left foreground. (Courtesy of Glen Dawson.)

Two unidentified members of the Johnston family pose at the south side of 1191 Mar Vista Avenue. The Johnston family owned the house until the early 1970s. Charles Johnston (1883–1968) was an attorney. Both he and his wife, Isabelle (1885–1971), were from Maine, where they were married in 1907. They came to Pasadena around 1913. (Courtesy of Glen Dawson.)

BUNGALOW PLAN NO. 406

Edward A. Daniell (1893–1976) was the most prolific developer in Bungalow Heaven, building 30 houses between 1916 and 1925. He lived in the neighborhood from 1922 to 1926. His specialty here was developing small lots on the east-west cross streets. His first bungalows in the neighborhood were 1226 Mar Vista Avenue and, in the rear of the lot, 1065 East Claremont Street, pictured in Telling's *Select California Bungalows*. (JdlC.)

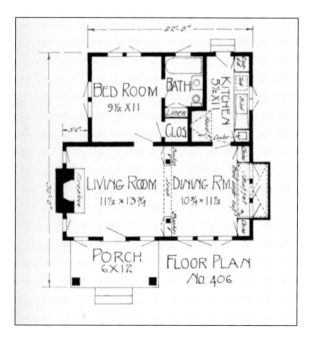

Edward Daniell's 1065 East Claremont Street cottage had a compact floor plan that typified the small dwellings he built here. It was erected for $1,300 in the spring of 1916 with Daniell acting as both owner and builder, as he did on all his projects. The designer was Pasadena contractor Asa C. Parlee (1885– ?), who might have assisted the inexperienced 23-year-old Daniell with the construction. (JdlC.)

46

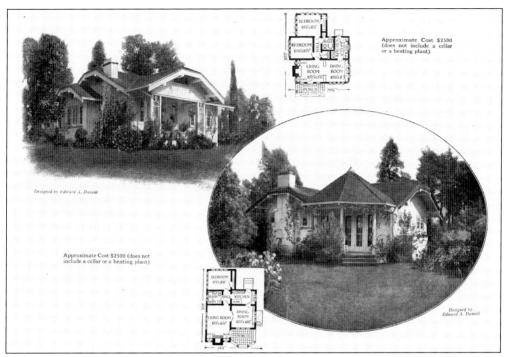

Approximate Cost $2500
(does not include a cellar
or a heating plant)

Approximate Cost $2500 (does not
include a cellar or a heating plant)

Designed by Edward A. Daniell

Designed by
Edward A. Daniell

Edward Daniell was able to get several of his Bungalow Heaven houses published. The one at 1065 East Claremont Street appeared in the 1916 edition of *Journal Bungalows*. Four subsequent Claremont cottages were included in the 1920 edition. This page from the latter used Flag Studio photographs with fake backgrounds of lush foliage. Pictured are 1027 and 974 East Claremont. (Ripley collection.)

The bungalow at 1027 East Claremont Street was one of four cottages initiated in November 1916 by Edward Daniell; it cost $1,650 and contained five rooms. Daniell took credit as the designer, but given his inexperience, he might have obtained help from a draftsman or architect functioning as a "ghost designer." The picturesque revival style of these cottages anticipates the storybook houses of the 1920s. (CSL.)

The bungalow at 1035 East Claremont Street, next door to the preceding cottage, was built at the same time as its neighbor for $1,500. After initially serving as an Edward Daniell rental, it was sold to Margaret Robinson in 1920. The half-octagon porch was a feature used on two other 1916 Daniell cottages. As can be seen here, even these small houses had automobile garages. (CSL.)

Four Edward Daniell cottages in a row were started in November 1916, and 1041 East Claremont Street was the third. It cost $1,400 and might have been called Colonial at the time, although the opening of the attic dormer vent is the only feature that is clearly Colonial. Visible on the right side is the bump out for a disappearing bed. (CSL.)

The fourth November 1916 Edward Daniell cottage built was 1049 East Claremont Street at a cost of $1,300. Like the house on 1041 East Claremont, it had four rooms and featured an imitation thatched roof, pointing to an English or European stylistic influence. This type of roof was not unusual for the period: the Greenes and the Heinemans both used this effect in 1912 designs. (CSL.)

Edward Daniell started another group of four revival cottages on East Claremont Street in December 1916. This group encompassed 958 through 982 East Claremont. Shown here is 958, which was constructed for $1,800, making it the most expensive of the pre–World War I Claremont cottages. It combined a half-octagon porch and imitation thatched roof. (CSL.)

Edward Daniell's 974 East Claremont Street was similar to 958 but contained four rooms rather than five, reducing the cost to $1,500. This house was selected to appear in the 1920 edition of *Journal Bungalows*. In all, over 20 families are known to have lived here over the years. Daniell rented it out through 1924, and subsequent owners did likewise through the 1930s. (CSL.)

Children pose in front of 982 East Claremont Street, a $1,400 cottage that was the last of the 1916 Edward Daniel series. Daniel built 20 small bungalows in the neighborhood in the 1920s, mostly in a simplified Spanish style. He would become a leading developer of the 1930–1950 era in the San Gabriel Valley, pioneering in large tract developments and constructing over 900 homes by the early 1940s. (CSL.)

Three

CONTRACTORS AND SMALLER SPECULATIVE BUILDERS

One of the leading Pasadena contracting firms of the period was the Foss Designing and Building Company. Beginning in 1904 as a proprietorship of Robert Foss, it was reorganized in 1911 as a stock company with Foss as president and an architectural staff. This advertisement from the 1912 city directory features a rendering of the Foss-built home at 1095 North Hill Street (discussed further on page 54). (PMH.)

Blue Prints and Specifications — FREE — Where Contract is Secured
Both Phones 209

Foss Designing & Building Co.
INCORPORATED
General Contractors

R. F. FOSS, Manager   Rooms 6-7-8
HOMES BUILT   100 East Colorado Street
On the Easy Payment Plan   Pasadena, Cal.

Robert Francis Foss (1869–1951) poses in his office in the Foss Designing and Building Company headquarters at 45 North Euclid Avenue, probably in the mid-1920s. Foss, a descendant of Danish immigrants who came to America in the 1650s, was the tenth generation of his family to be born in New Hampshire. He went into carpentry and took correspondence courses in making house plans. Relocating to Pasadena in 1903, he quickly became a successful builder and contractor. He constructed about 100 houses in Pasadena between 1904 and 1911, and the successor corporation built another 70 or so houses before 1918, remaining successful through the 1920s. He retired in 1928 and sold the company. The firm was subsequently sold to the Judson family in 1932, and then to the Teal family in 1985, and remains in business today as a termite control company. (HL.)

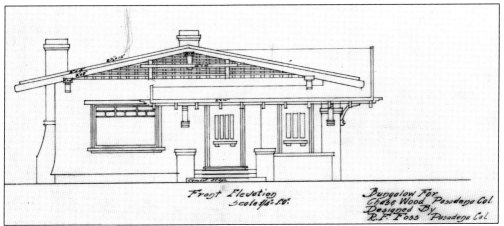

Front Elevation
Scale 1/4"=1'0"

Bungalow For
Chase Wood Pasadena Cal.
Designed By
R.F. Foss Pasadena Cal

R.F. Foss designed and built 1205 North Michigan Avenue for Chase Wood in 1911, just before the Foss Designing and Building Company was incorporated. It contained five rooms and cost $2,617, considered substantial for a home of its size. The design essentially duplicates that of 510 North Madison Avenue, Foss's own house, which was built just prior to this one. (HL.)

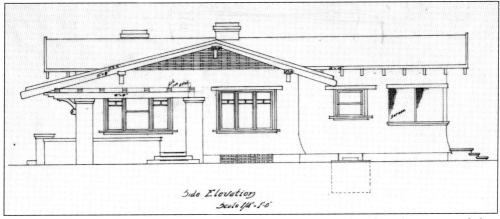

Side Elevation
Scale 1/4"=1'0"

The side elevation of the Chase Wood bungalow shows the "railroad track" pattern of glass window panes that became a Foss hallmark in the Craftsman period. The curved knee braces were another typical Foss detail. The cut-in porch shown in the plans was mostly enclosed by later owners. (HL.)

The house at 1095 North Hill Avenue was constructed by Foss for Wallace Woodworth in late 1911 at a cost of $4,965. This was the first home commissioned by the firm J.H. Woodworth and Son on the land that became Tract 1945 (see chapter five). Although just outside of the Bungalow Heaven Landmark District boundary, the houses on the west side of Hill were really part of the same neighborhood. (HL.)

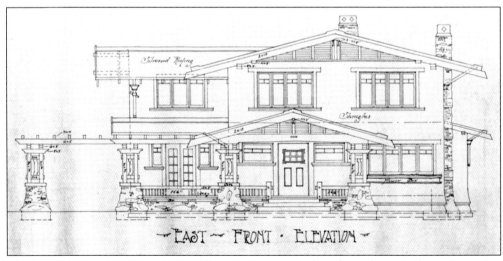

The front elevation of 1095 North Hill Avenue varies slightly from the as-built configuration shown in the preceding photograph. The 1912 Foss advertisement (page 51) matches the plans. The head of the Foss Designing and Building Company's architectural department from mid-1911 to mid-1913 was Harry Monroe Banfield (1877–1941), a licensed architect who had worked in prestigious offices such as Greene and Greene, Hunt and Grey, and Frederick L. Roehrig. (HL.)

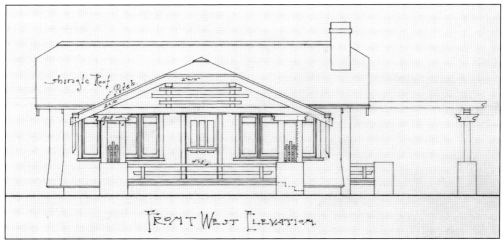

John Keith was a Foss client for three houses in Bungalow Heaven. The first was 722 Mar Vista Avenue, constructed in 1913 for $2,500; the design was presumably by Harry Banfield. The Foss Designing and Building Company returned in 1917 to make alterations and additions at the rear, creating an additional living room and an additional kitchen to form a duplex. (HL.)

This retouched photograph of 722 Mar Vista Avenue appeared in *Ladies Home Journal* in 1915 and its *Journal Bungalows* plan book in 1916, 1920, and 1921. Some variations between the plans and the house as built include a different treatment of the porch gable, a shortening of the side pergola, and a different front door. Minor changes were commonly made during construction. (Ripley collection.)

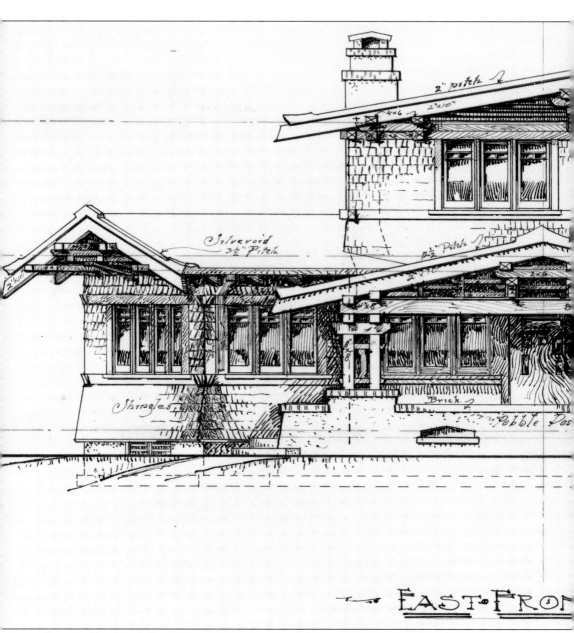

EAST·FRON

Retirees Frank and Oretha Lemon commissioned the Foss Designing and Building Company to erect 815 North Holliston Avenue in 1912 for $4,218. The Lemons remained here until 1926. William and Marion Pankey were the owners from 1939 to 1958. Marion Pankey had a dressmaking business, Marion Originals, located at the house from 1955 to 1958. In this design, Harry Banfield created an unusual variation of the chalet type by placing canted wings at the front corners.

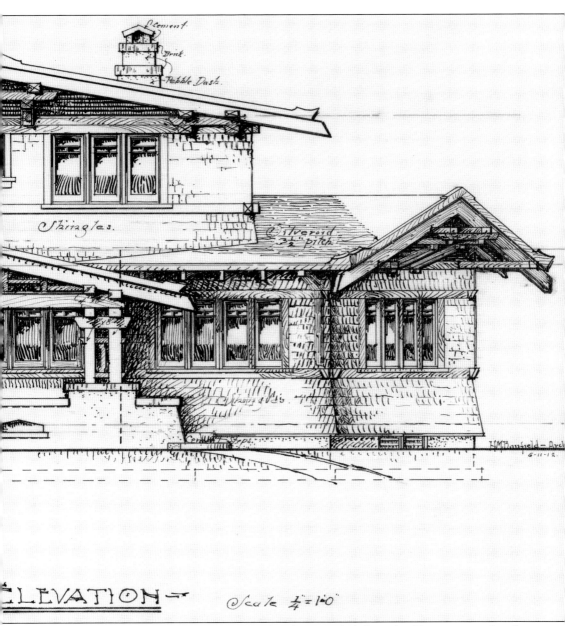

ELEVATION — Scale ¼"=1'-0"

Besides the "railroad track" windows mentioned earlier, it included another Foss signature detail in the form of stacked timbers in the gables, also seen in the Chase Wood bungalow. This front elevation was shaded and detailed to become a presentation drawing; Banfield's signature is visible on the right at ground level. (HL.)

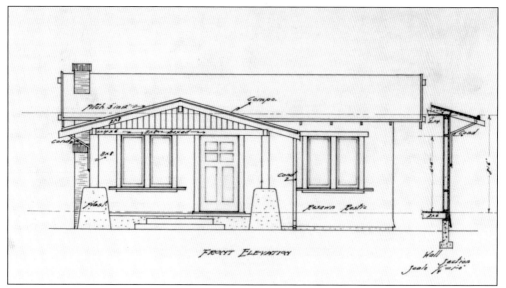

This tiny three-room bungalow at 795 Mar Vista Avenue was the second designed by the Foss Designing and Building Company for John Keith, who acted as the builder when it was constructed in 1914 for $1,400. A large front addition doubled its size and removed the front elevation in 1953. It was sited at the rear of the lot, leaving room for a future house that was never built. (HL.)

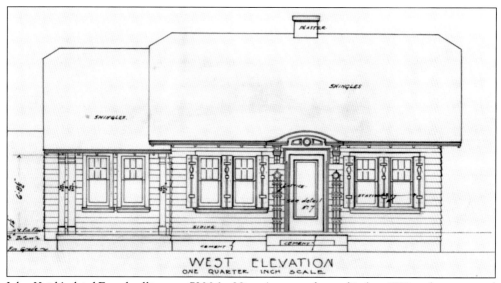

John Keith's third Foss dwelling was 730 Mar Vista Avenue, planned in late 1920 and constructed in 1921 for $4,000, with Keith acting as the builder. This four-room Colonial bungalow illustrates how styles had changed in the seven years since 722 Mar Vista was completed. The cut-in porch on the left was enclosed some time after 1930. (HL.)

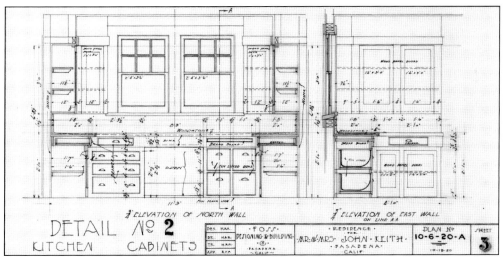

This drawing of the kitchen details for 730 Mar Vista Avenue shows typical period features such as a "woodstone" composition countertop and an open area below the sink. The title block shows the designer as "HAR." These are the initials of Herman A. Reuter (1885–1933), who took over as the head of the Foss architectural department in 1920. (HL.)

The front entrance details for 730 Mar Vista Avenue illustrate careful design, even on a small job. The as-built house reflects some changes, probably to reduce the cost. The title block indicates that this sheet was designed by Herman A. Reuter and traced by Earll C. Weaver, a civil engineer who later became the Foss Designing and Building Company's assistant general manager. (HL.)

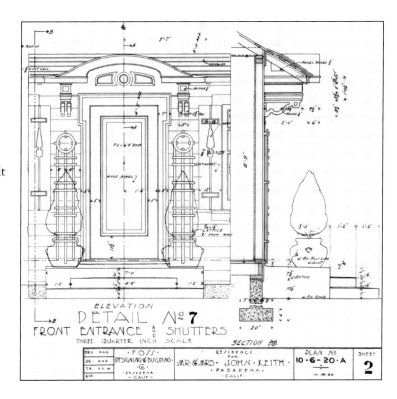

This Foss Designing and Building Company interior illustration was published in a company brochure. The location is unknown, but it is included here as a representative interior. Historical interior photographs of actual Bungalow Heaven houses are uncommon. This view shows typical features, such as simple stained woodwork, tiled fireplace, Arts and Crafts wallpaper, early electric lighting fixtures, sheer curtains, and Mission furniture. (HL.)

David Malcolm Renton (1878–1947) was one of Pasadena's leading builders during the Craftsman period. A native of Prince Edward Island, Canada, he went to Massachusetts in the late 1890s, worked as a carpenter, and began contracting on his arrival in Pasadena in 1902. His prolific design-build firm continued until 1919, when he became general manager of the Santa Catalina Island Company. (Courtesy of City of Pasadena.)

David Renton built his first Bungalow Heaven house in 1910, but the earliest to appear in a historical photograph was 1155 North Michigan Avenue, constructed in early 1913. Designed by Renton, it was built for Jessie Gilman at a cost of $2,400. The Greene and Greene touches in Renton's designs undoubtedly drew from his experience as the contractor for 10 Greene and Greene homes between 1902 and 1908. (FS-PMH 2-49-266.)

David Renton's 945 North Holliston Avenue was the first of four bungalows he designed and built for J.H. Woodworth and Son as speculative houses in their new tract (see chapter five). It was erected in mid-1913 for $3,200. In the background is the bungalow at 965 North Holliston, designed by Renton but constructed by the Woodworth firm for David Zook in 1914. (FS-PMH 2-49-176.)

The next David Renton design-build project for the Woodworths was the bungalow at 945 North Chester Avenue, constructed in the fall of 1913 for $3,100. The Woodworths aimed at an upper middle-class clientele, so these houses on the east side of the neighborhood cost about 50 percent more than the smaller bungalows on the west. Many of the Renton designs built in Bungalow Heaven, including this one, had *L*-shaped porches. (FS-PMH 2-49-119.)

The bungalow at 976 North Chester Avenue was designed and built for J.H. Woodworth and Son in late 1913 at a cost of $3,500. Evident here was David Renton's fondness for using multiple gables in his Craftsman designs. The stonework is particularly well executed. Beside the rear driveway is a low wire-mesh fence. Such fences were common during the period, as were wood fences of square lattice. (FS-PMH 2-49-121.)

Built for the Woodworths at the same time as 976 North Chester Avenue, this stucco bungalow at 985 North Chester cost $3,500. The style was probably intended to be Prairie or Italian Renaissance. Many Italian designs of the 1910s were strongly rectilinear and had a Prairie flavor, but here the lack of classical details tips the design toward the Prairie style. The bungalow at 1018 North Michigan appears in the right background. (FS-PMH 2-49-122.)

Renton's last house in Bungalow Heaven was 1218 North Michigan Avenue, designed and constructed in 1915 for Harvey H. Vincent at a cost of $2,500. The influence of the Colonial Revival style seems apparent in the symmetrical facade and the comparatively refined scale of the structural elements, although the design does not attempt to duplicate historical Colonial structures. (CSL.)

Charles Twombly (1860–1936) built this speculative bungalow at 1245 East Orange Grove Boulevard in 1911 for $2,000. Twombly moved his building business from Alhambra to Pasadena around 1910, and he built eight houses in Bungalow Heaven between 1911 and 1914. Though he is known to have designed some of his houses, there is no documentation regarding the designer of this one. (FS-PMH 2-49-287.)

Charles Twombly designed and built 1019 North Michigan Avenue for $1,500 in late 1912 as a speculative venture. This particular design was very successful for him, and he built it four more times through 1913. The design featured multiple gables with many wings and bays. The wide porch had a pergola overhead instead of the more usual roof. (FS-PMH 2-49-262.)

Charles Twombly's 1277 North Michigan Avenue bungalow was constructed for the Chester R. Pyle real estate firm in 1913 at a cost of $1,800. It was Twombly's last use of the design first constructed at 1019 North Michigan. The front door of this one featured a window in the form of a crescent moon. (FS-PMH 2-49-271.)

Walter A. Waldock (1864–1950) was a carpenter, contractor, and speculative builder who put up at least 25 houses in Pasadena between 1904 and 1923. He concentrated on Bungalow Heaven starting in 1908. The bungalow at 1281 North Catalina Avenue, shown here, was built in 1912 for $2,200. It featured masonry of mixed stone and clinker brick, sometimes referred to as the "peanut brittle" style because of its appearance. (FS-PMH 2-49-118.)

Walter Waldock erected 1045 East Orange Grove Boulevard on speculation for $2,000 in 1913. He repeated this basic design, which featured a pop-up "airplane room" on the roof, at 1271 Mar Vista Avenue and 1207 North Wilson Avenue in 1913. The type of fence shown in this photograph was very popular during the period. (FS-PMH 2-49-285.)

This exemplary Japo-Swiss bungalow at 1165 North Michigan Avenue was built on speculation in early 1912 for $2,200 by Kieft and Hetherington, who built a "twin" at 815 North Mentor Avenue (shown on the cover). The Pasadena firm dealt in wholesale chemicals and had a sideline in home building. The designs of its bungalows were usually credited to the firm on surviving building permits, but the sophistication suggests use of an unidentified "ghost designer." (FS-PMH 2-49-267.)

The bungalow at 1299 North Michigan Avenue was also constructed by Kieft and Hetherington on speculation in 1912 at a cost of $2,500. A child rides a tricycle on the driveway in this 1914 photograph. To the right is the bungalow at 1309 North Michigan, another Kieft and Hetherington bungalow from 1912. Altogether, the firm built seven houses in Bungalow Heaven. (FS-PMH 2-49-273.)

This final Kieft and Hetherington bungalow at 1089 North Chester Avenue was built on speculation in 1913 for $3,500. Senior firm member Henry J. Hetherington (1856–1927) was born in Scotland and came to the United States in 1881. Around 1904, Henry's daughter married William Kieft, who was born in 1882 to Dutch immigrants in Michigan. They founded the firm in 1907 when they arrived in Pasadena. (FS-PMH 2-49-127.)

The bungalow at 850 North Chester Avenue was the last of five bungalows constructed in the neighborhood in 1911 by South Pasadena contractor John G. Pierce (1872– ?). It was built on speculation for $2,500. Pierce was a documented house designer and may have designed this one. A Michigan native, he came to California before 1900 and went into building in 1906. He left the area around 1917 for Birmingham, Alabama. (Ripley collection.)

This $2,500 bungalow was the third of four speculative houses built between 1907 and 1911 by William Summers (1867–1938), a real estate broker and developer who also owned a glove factory. It was constructed at 749 Mar Vista Avenue in late 1910, with Summers acting as the builder. The design was published as plan no. 1312 in *Sweet's Bungalows*, a 1912 plan book by South Pasadenan Edward Sweet. (FS-PMH 2-49-224.)

In 1911, William Summers used the same design as the preceding for 715 North Michigan Avenue. It was constructed by contractor John Burkett Pierce (1873–1961) at a cost of $2,750. The only noticeable difference from 749 Mar Vista Avenue was the pergola over the driveway. Both houses exemplified an often-used feature of the era: a flaring stucco skirt below a windowsill-level waistband. (FS-PMH 2-49-248.)

Pasadena real estate dealer Harry H. Godber (1868–1936) commissioned 11 speculative houses in the neighborhood from various contractors between 1913 and 1923; this bungalow at 1275 North Mentor Avenue was one of the first. It was built by William J. Seaton in late 1913 for $2,400. In the background is 1285 North Mentor, a 1909 speculative bungalow by contractor Henry C. Deming. (FS-PMH 2-49-241.)

Roscoe J. McMillin (1885–1958) worked for various Pasadena plumbing businesses from 1903 until about 1947. He built houses as a sideline from 1911 until the Depression, sometimes living in them until they sold. Six of these are in Bungalow Heaven, including 1241 North Chester Avenue, built in 1913 for $2,500. McMillin claimed design credit for some 1920s houses, so it is possible that he designed earlier ones. (FS-PMH 2-49-128.)

Pasadenan Irvin Benjamin Speicher (1889–1933) built 12 speculative houses in Bungalow Heaven between 1913 and 1920. An Indiana native of Swiss heritage, he continued as a builder until about 1925 and later became a stockbroker. The bungalow at 1094 North Michigan Avenue, pictured here in 1931, cost $6,500 in late 1920. Though built after World War I, its design continues the pre-war Arts and Crafts aesthetic in simpler form. (FS-PMH 2-49-264.)

Four

FAMILY-BUILT HOMES STREET BY STREET

While developers and speculators built about half of Bungalow Heaven's houses, individuals or families commissioned the other half. Family pride radiates from this photograph showing off the new home, automobile, and dogs of Stephen and Bertha Shaljian at 775 North Mentor Avenue. They hired Mead and Nelson to construct it in 1913 for $4,000. The designer was Pasadena draftsman and builder William C. Leonardi. (Ripley collection.)

Another bungalow on North Mentor Avenue was this one at 734, built in 1912 for L.A. Webb by contractors McLin and Green at a cost of $2,500. A second story was added in 1919 by the Foss Designing and Building Company, but this early image shows the house as originally built. A portion of 726 North Mentor, built in 1914, is seen on the right. (FS-PMH 2-49-330.)

Catalina Avenue houses included this 1921 bungalow erected at 730 North Catalina Avenue for $2,250 by Myron and Anna Lance, the owners and builders. In this 1922 photograph, their daughter Fern Welch sits in front of the house with her baby daughter Audrey and three-year-old son Harry. The Lances came to California from Kansas. (Courtesy of Dennis Bedford.)

The 1908 home at 805 North Catalina Avenue was constructed at a cost of $1,550 by Theodore C. Pearce for furniture store owner Jasper N. Humphreys and his wife, Eva. From 1936 until 1961, it was the home of George and Louise Rice and their family. This view was probably taken in the 1950s. (Courtesy of Tom and Cindy Rice.)

Newspaper boy and Longfellow student Kenneth Frederick Rice (right) and pal John Mosely are in front of the Rice family's bungalow at 805 North Catalina Avenue. Ken's father, a painter and paperhanger, bought it with the help of Ken's grandfather for $3,000. Ken's son Tom and wife, Cindy, live in a beautifully restored Craftsman they own on Michigan Avenue. (Courtesy of Tom and Cindy Rice.)

Ken Rice lived in his family's home on Catalina until 1955. A USC graduate, he taught history at Pasadena's John Muir High School from 1957 to 1986. In a piece written for the 1998 *Home Tour*, he remembered the 1930s: streetcars on Lake Avenue, its corner soda fountain, and the neighborhood being "a good place for a kid to grow up." (Courtesy of Tom and Cindy Rice.)

The bungalow at 811 North Catalina Avenue was constructed for Frederick and Ruby Abbott by Jonas R. Slater in late 1917 at a cost of $1,650. Frederick owned a tailor shop in downtown Pasadena. Only 118 houses were built in the entire city in 1917 because World War I virtually halted home building. This snapshot shows the house in 1929. (PMH H1-78.)

Augustus Dorman commissioned Harry O. Clark to construct 1177 North Catalina Avenue in early 1911 for $2,400. Dorman was the father-in-law and former business partner of George A. Clark (1871–1940), a Pasadena men's clothier who took up architecture as a hobby. It seems likely that Clark designed this stylish bungalow. He took part in the 1913 Los Angeles Architectural Club exhibition, demonstrating that "real" architects respected his abilities. (FS-PMH 2-49-116.)

Neighborhood contractor Sherman Seeds built 1263 North Catalina Avenue for blacksmith Thomas Davis and his wife, Lotta, in 1913 at a cost of $2,800. In this 1914 photograph, both 1263 and its neighbor 1271 show the classic Craftsman exterior scheme of dark walls, even darker trim, and light-toned sash and screen frames. (FS-PMH 2-49-117.)

On Wilson Avenue, Agnes Burr commissioned 1131 from contractors Edgar Bell and John Powell in early 1914 for $1,800. She was a writer with a syndicated newspaper column on women's fashions and had several books to her credit. She used the house primarily as a rental, eventually selling it to Horton (1874–1939) and Anna (1886–1971) Jennison in 1920. (Courtesy of Marilyn Jennison Lucht.)

The Jennison family retained ownership of 1131 North Wilson Avenue until 1988. A recent photograph shows that the house has seen few changes during its existence. A lighter color scheme, a porch railing, and the screening of the side porch are the only noticeable exterior changes. This is a typical example representing the high level of historical integrity found in the neighborhood. (Photograph by James Staub.)

This early view captures the built-in seat and bookcases in the living room of 1131 North Wilson Avenue. James Jennison (1911–2004), who grew up here, constructed an elaborate model town in the backyard, winning a prize from a toy manufacturer for the best model railroad by a boy under 12. He later graduated from Caltech and became a structural engineer for the Navy. (Courtesy of Marilyn Jennison Lucht.)

Walter S. Houseworth constructed 1225 North Wilson Avenue in late 1911 and lived here until 1914. He owned the Houseworth Building Company from 1911 to 1913. While he only built four other houses, he claimed credit as the designer for one of them. He may have also designed this $2,000 bungalow, which takes advantage of its corner site with a wraparound pergola porch. (FS-PMH 2-49-328.)

Shown during construction in 1923 is 1282 North Wilson Avenue, one of the first Pasadena buildings by Arthur G. Gehrig (1887–1970), a civil engineer and contractor. Neil and Lena Haffner commissioned it for $5,700. Gehrig became a Pasadena City College engineering teacher in 1929. Named Teacher of the Year in 1950, he retired in 1953 and lived at 1272 Wilson until 1961. (Courtesy of Bungalow Heaven Neighborhood Association.)

Insurance broker Frank Fawkes (1867–1956) and his wife, Ulla (1866–1952), hired Frank Crosby to build 1290 North Wilson Avenue in 1913 for $2,300. Their daughter Miriam continued to live here until her death in 1999. Visible in the background is 1298 North Wilson, built by and for John R. Lind in 1914 at a cost of $2,300. The preceding photograph shows another view of 1290. (FS-PMH 2-49-329.)

The views of family-built bungalows on Mar Vista Avenue begin with this 1948 photograph of 1135 East Orange Grove Boulevard (at the corner of Mar Vista). Robert and Martha Douglas hired the Aetna Bond and Mortgage Company to build this Spanish Revival–style bungalow for $4,500 at the end of 1922. A rear house at 709 Mar Vista, built at the same time, is just visible. (JAH-PMH Hawkins-3351.)

Daniel Whetstine (1874–1955) lived at 1076 Mar Vista Avenue from 1915 to 1920. A prominent builder, he rarely ventured into speculation; however, in 1919 he was the owner-builder of 1061 Mar Vista, shown here. It became the home of Emmett B. Norman, an orange grower, and his wife, Viola. In this c. 1921 snapshot, E.B. Norman stands in the front near an automobile. (Courtesy of Sidney Gally.)

Posing in the driveway of 1061 Mar Vista Avenue (then named Stevenson Avenue) during a visit around 1921 are, from left to right, Lillian, Thomas, and son Sidney Gally, who later became a longtime resident and a founder of the neighborhood association. Lillian Gally was the daughter of E.B. and Viola Norman, the owners at that time. The house remains in the family. (Courtesy of Sidney Gally.)

This bungalow at 1095 Mar Vista Avenue was constructed in late 1913 for Jacob and Della Probst at a cost of $1,800. The builder (and possible designer) was Jacob's brother Marentius A. "Monte" Probst (1879–1966), a well-established contractor in South Pasadena and surrounding areas from about 1908 until World War II. The Probst family came to the United States from Denmark in 1884. Jacob was a house painter. (PMH H11-13A.)

Between 1914 and 1917, Hans W. Larsen (1867–1953) built two bungalows on a lot he owned at Mar Vista Avenue and Claremont Street. This property was the only speculative venture by Larsen, a builder who came to America from Denmark in 1898. The main house (1227 Mar Vista) was built in early 1917 for $3,000 using plans by George Telling. It appeared in his *Select California Bungalows* in 1921. (JdlC.)

BUNGALOW PLAN NO. 522

The Larsen bungalow at the rear of 1227 Mar Vista Avenue has the address 1115 East Claremont Street. While the main house tended toward the Colonial style, this one from only three years earlier was typically Craftsman. It may have been designed by Larsen, who built it in 1914 for $1,100. This view, with a fake background, is from Telling's 1921 book *Select California Bungalows*. (JdlC.)

Designed by Cyril Bennett

Harley Andrews was the owner and builder of 1302 Mar Vista Avenue, which cost $2,400 in early 1914. This was the first completed building by architect Cyril Bennett after he left Sylvanus Marston's firm and opened his own office. Marston was an early proponent of the Colonial-style bungalow, and Bennett closely follows Marston's lead here. This image appeared in *Ladies Home Journal* and *Journal Bungalows* in 1916. (Ripley collection.)

Contractor John Burkett Pierce built this stylish airplane bungalow for Margaret Anderson in early 1912 for $3,500. The original address of 697 North Michigan Avenue was changed later to 1185 East Orange Grove Boulevard. Its designer is unidentified, although it has an exterior window apron design that was a signature detail of Arthur and Alfred Heineman. In the foreground is what appears to be a streetcar-waiting bench. (FS-PMH 2-49-286.)

The bungalow at 745 North Michigan Avenue was constructed by John Burkett Pierce for Edwin Rose in 1914 at a cost of $2,000. It displays the lighter exterior palette of the middle and later 1910s. Pierce built nine bungalows in Pasadena during the pre–World War I period. He designed his own house in 1912 and could possibly have been the designer of this one. (FS-PMH 2-49-250.)

Charles and Ellen Bradley were the owners and builders of 752 North Michigan Avenue, shown here as it appeared in an article by Helen Lukens Gaut in Stickley's *Craftsman* magazine in November 1910. It cost $2,000 to build in 1909. The Bradleys were retirees from the Chicago area. Many of Bungalow Heaven's early residents were retirees from the Midwest. (PPL.)

This striking 1914 bungalow at 986 North Michigan Avenue was built at a cost of $2,300 by Manson O. Sanford for bank cashier Henry P. Thayer. George Telling gave the design a full page (showing a twin) in his 1921 plan book *Select California Bungalows*. Telling did not claim design credit but described it as "radical enough to attract much favorable attention even in Pasadena." (FS-PMH 2-49-259.)

Clarence M. Gregg, a hardware store owner, commissioned this bungalow at 1166 North Michigan Avenue in early 1913 for $2,400. The builder was Charles Twombly, while the design was by another builder, William Paget (1861–1929). Gregg sold it in 1914 to Richard and Cecilia Luckey. Richard's sister Gertrude and her husband, Frank Waldron, lived here in 1919. This retouched photograph appeared in *Ladies Home Journal* in January 1916. (PPL.)

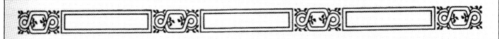

$3,000 Bungalow Has Its Porch and Pergola Decked Out in Tracery of Roses

(By GERTRUDE APPLETON LUCKEY)

 **W**ITH dainty roses and twining vines growing over its columned pergola and the graceful lines of the design showing through a delicate tracery of foliage, there is unusual charm about this six-room bungalow. Designed by William Paget, the home is located in the northeastern section of Pasadena, California.

Gertrude Luckey (later Waldron; 1888–1980) was a frequent contributor to home-building magazines in the late 1910s and early 1920s. She lived with her parents and siblings at 1182 North Michigan Avenue from 1915 through 1918, moving to 1166 North Michigan when she married around 1919. This image shows the beginning of a long article on the Luckey home that appeared in *Bungalow Magazine* in December 1916. (JdlC.)

This Front View Indicates the Homelike Simplicity and Architectural Beauty of the General Design

This exterior view of 1182 North Michigan Avenue was part of Luckey's 1916 article. The house was designed and built as a speculative venture by William Paget, who also designed 1166, as discussed above. The bungalow at 1182 North Michigan contained six rooms and cost $2,000 to build in mid-1914. The Luckeys were apparently the original purchasers. (JdlC.)

The Living Room Stretches Across the Front of the House and Has South and West Exposures

The living room of 1182 North Michigan Avenue is shown here as it appeared in the Luckey article of 1916. It was described in part as follows: "The walls are tinted a shade of dark tan. The woodwork is Oregon pine stained brown and finished with a dull polish. The fireplace of green tile is at one end of the room." (JdlC.)

Two Bookcases, Slightly More Than Five Feet High, Separate the Dining Room From the Living Room

Gertrude Luckey's 1916 article included this photograph of the dining room of 1182 North Michigan Avenue. She wrote, "The dining room walls are paneled up to the plate rail which is five feet over the floor. The paneling is made of twelve-inch boards of Oregon pine. . . . The color scheme of this room is the same as that of the living room." (JdlC.)

Luckey described the kitchen of 1182 North Michigan Avenue, illustrated here, as having a "woodstone" composition countertop that was three feet above the floor. Visible is a typical large single sink with separate hot- and cold-water taps. Kitchens were usually painted in light colors during the Arts and Crafts period. (JdlC.)

Here is a Practical Well Lighted Sink and Kitchen

Oregon Pine, Finished in Ivory Enamel, is Used in Bedrooms, Which Have Pink and White Wall Paper

This photograph of a bedroom of 1182 North Michigan Avenue appeared in the Luckey article and was described as follows: "The woodwork is of Oregon pine finished in ivory enamel. The walls are papered with striped paper in white and pink. The border of pink roses makes it attractive. The closet door has a plate glass mirror." (JdlC.)

Robert Baxter Burhans (1853–1946) was the owner and builder of record for 1191 North Michigan Avenue, which cost $2,500 to construct in 1911. Burhans was a retired widower from New York. A swinging lounge chair made of cloth can be seen on the front porch in this 1914 view. (FS-PMH 2-49-268.)

The bungalow at 1260 North Michigan Avenue was built by Melville A. Hester for Harvey and Etta Vincent in late 1912 at a cost of $2,400. The Vincents had migrated in the 1880s from Wisconsin to Los Angeles, where Harvey became a freight agent. They retired to Pasadena and lived at 1260 North Michigan Avenue until Etta's death in 1919. They built four other houses nearby during the 1910s. (FS-PMH 2-49-269.)

Mary Bailey hired Harry O. Clarke to design and build this airplane bungalow at 1291 North Michigan Avenue for $3,700 in early 1913. A widow, she lived here with her daughter and two sisters. The plan is a south-facing U, providing light and views to the core of the house. Clarke (1880–1941) was in the contracting business in Pasadena from 1911 to 1941. (FS-PMH 2-49-272.)

The bungalow at 1325 North Michigan Avenue (later changed to 1194 East Washington Boulevard) was one of the few Mission-style houses built in Bungalow Heaven. The Mission style, a predecessor of Spanish Colonial, often included Arts and Crafts features. This $5,100 airplane bungalow with pop-up rooms was constructed in 1913 for William C. Francis by Harry Clarke. George Costerisan and Frank Kavanaugh of Los Angeles were the architects. (FS-PMH 2-49-325.)

Images of Chester Avenue family-commissioned homes begin with 1273 East Orange Grove Boulevard on the corner of North Chester Avenue. This Colonial bungalow was designed and built by William C. Leonardi in 1917 for Harry and Nellie Stanberry at a cost of $2,700. The Stanberrys were retirees from Iowa, where he had been a schoolteacher. (CSL.)

Sherman Seeds built 771 North Chester Avenue for his own use in 1919 for $4,500. He and his wife, Mary, lived here until 1933. Seeds (1865–1957) came to Pasadena about 1905 and worked as a carpenter. He became an independent building contractor in 1910, constructing several other houses in Bungalow Heaven in the 1910s. Seeds sometimes designed the homes he built, including possibly this one. (Photograph by James Staub.)

Bungalow kitchens were designed to be utilitarian: simple and useful with plenty of space, storage, and good equipment, as well as being well ventilated and full of sunshine. The kitchen at 771 North Chester Avenue is typical but unusual in that the original built-in wooden cabinetry shown here had a natural finish. In most period kitchens, the cabinetry was painted white, which was thought to be more sanitary. (Photograph by James Staub.)

Swedish-born Oscar and Bertha Youngren, who lived at 771 North Chester Avenue with their daughters Margarita, Linnea, and Thelma, are shown during Christmastime in the late 1940s. Although the house has seen several owners and many renters, the living room with its Douglas fir woodwork and iron-spot brick fireplace has remained intact, as has the kitchen cabinetry. (Courtesy of Terry Hartley and James Staub.)

On January 11, 1949, the heaviest snowstorm in Southern California history blanketed Pasadena, a city whose reputation was built on its sunny winter skies (see page 110). Here, the Youngrens are enjoying the Arctic weather on their lawn at 771 North Chester Avenue. The bungalow at 763 North Chester (on the left) was built by Sherman Seeds in 1913 for $2,300. (Courtesy of Terry Hartley and James Staub.)

BUNGALOW PLAN NO. 618

The bungalow at 865 North Chester Avenue was constructed for $2,000 at the end of 1911 by William Erickson for his sister Josephine Erickson, who used it as a rental. William Erickson (1871–1953) was born in Sweden and came to the United States in 1890. Starting in 1910, he was in business here as a carpenter and occasional builder. This retouched image is from George Telling's *Select California Bungalows* (1921). (JdlC.)

Five

WOODWORTHS AND FRIENDS

Tract no. 1945, often called the Woodworth Tract, was platted in 1913 by the Pasadena real estate firm J. H. Woodworth and Son. Covering 40 acres in what was then the far northeast corner of Pasadena, the tract was publicized as being the largest single subdivision in the city up to that time. Most of the tract had been part of Barney Williams's ranch. (Courtesy of City of Pasadena.)

TRACT Nº 1945

The Woodworth Tract runs from Mountain Street north to about 1170 on Chester Avenue, Holliston Avenue, and the west side of Hill Avenue. This view looking north on Chester from Mountain was taken around 1919, when development was about to resume after World War I. Note the utilitarian streetlight and young street trees. (CSL.)

A major storm caused flooding and washouts on Holliston Avenue just below Mountain Street in 1914. Beyond the damaged area is the Woodworth Tract, almost all vacant. The Woodworth firm was established by Judson H. Woodworth (1845–1938) during the boom of 1886. His son Wallace S. Woodworth (1877–1947) became his partner in 1903 after graduating from Pomona College. (FS-PMH 2-75-105.)

The tracts between the Woodworth Tract and Washington Boulevard were subdivided at about the same time as the Woodworth Tract and were similar to it but smaller. This c. 1921 view west on Washington shows the intersection of Holliston and, in the background, houses on Chester Avenue just below Washington. (HL.)

After hiring D.M. Renton to build several bungalows in 1913, the Woodworths opened a building and contracting department in 1914. They commissioned young Pasadena architect Cyril Bennett (1891–1957) to make plans for about 10 bungalows to be built in their tract. The first to be started was this Craftsman-Colonial bungalow at 1036 North Chester Avenue, pictured here in late 1914. (FS-PMH 2-49-124.)

Designed by Cyril Bennett

This view of 1036 North Chester Avenue is from the *Ladies Home Journal* bungalow plan book of 1916. Construction began in April 1914 and was estimated at $3,490 (including the garage), much more than the $1,500 to $2,500 cost range for typical Bungalow Heaven homes to the west. The Woodworths advertised their tract with an eye toward upper-middle-class clients. (Ripley collection.)

The bungalow at 1053 North Chester Avenue was started at the same time as 1036. Another Cyril Bennett design, it also was estimated at $3,490. While 1036 was thought of as Colonial in style at the time, 1053 was solidly in the mainstream of the pure Craftsman style. The long porch with its massive tapered piers is strikingly assertive. (FS-PMH 2-49-125.)

The bungalow at 1025 North Chester Avenue was also started in April 1914, shortly after 1036 and 1053. Like the rest of the early Cyril Bennett houses for the Woodworths, it cost $3,490. This Japo-Swiss Craftsman bungalow was the home of Wallace Woodworth in 1915 and 1916. Note the Japanese–style (or Greene and Greene) lantern on the pier to the left of the steps. (FS-PMH 2-49-123.)

The next Woodworth-Bennett bungalow was 1080 North Chester Avenue, started in May 1914 and costing $3,490. Though thoroughly Japo-Swiss, it had the lighter colors typical of the mid-1910s onward. Neighborhood magazine writer Gertrude Luckey used this photograph in an article on the use of stonework in bungalows for the June 1916 issue of *Bungalow Magazine*. (FS-PMH 2-49-126.)

The Woodworth-Bennett series continued with 967 North Chester Avenue in July 1914. This Craftsman design featured hipped gables (jerkinheads) and masonry of mixed stone and stucco. A Woodworth "for sale" sign hangs from the porch beam in this late 1914 view. The Japo-Swiss Craftsman style was losing popularity around this time, and this house was the last of the style to be built by the Woodworths. (FS-PMH 2-49-120.)

Designed by Cyril Bennett

In October 1914, the Woodworths started another $3,490 Cyril Bennett–designed bungalow at 942 North Chester Avenue. The symmetrical facade and more delicate porch structure tend toward the Colonial-Craftsman blends of the 1910s, although there is nothing overtly Colonial here. This photograph was one of the illustrations in a *Ladies Home Journal* article in April 1916 titled "The New Colonial Bungalow." (Ripley collection.)

The only Cyril Bennett design built by the Woodworths on Holliston Avenue was 925, constructed in late 1914 for $4,000. It was similar to 1036 North Chester Avenue and another Bennett-Woodworth house at 1029 North Hill. Colonial-Craftsman in style, it was quite different from the formal Georgian Colonials that came to typify the Colonial style in the 1920s. (CSL.)

The Woodworths decided to add design capabilities to their firm in 1916. They hired a young draftsman named Kenneth Arthur Gordon to take charge of the new department. One of his early designs was 988 North Holliston Avenue, built in late 1916 for Woodworth client Frank Dunham for $4,500. It was another example of the Colonial-Craftsman style of the 1910s. (CSL.)

This Colonial Bungalow at 1150 North Chester Avenue was built by the Woodworths on speculation to Kenneth Gordon's design in early 1917 for $4,000. Gordon (1892–1966) had worked for architect Joseph Blick in 1912 and 1913; from 1913 to 1916, Gordon was a draftsperson for Reginald D. Johnson, one of the most respected and influential architects of the 1910–1940 period. This house shows similarities to Johnson's houses of the 1910s. (CSL.)

A second snapshot of 1150 North Chester Avenue shows the mountain view often touted in period advertisements. This symmetrical Colonial design reflects Craftsman influences in the grouped casement windows and the porches at each end. Houses such as this do not truly replicate early American forms but use borrowed design features to evoke the Colonial within a modified bungalow composition. (CSL.)

The Woodworths built this Kenneth Gordon–designed Colonial bungalow at 1070 North Chester Avenue on speculation for $3,500 in early 1917, just after completing 1150. While it shares many details with the latter, it is more Craftsman because of its asymmetrical layout, living porch, and porte cochere pergola. Gordon and the Woodworths were hired in 1929 to add a second floor for owner Dr. John Chapman at a cost of $5,000. (CSL.)

Another early 1917 Woodworth-Gordon speculative house was erected at 1020 North Holliston Avenue at a cost of $5,500. This one resembled 1150 North Chester Avenue but had stucco and a different roof treatment. The facade's design was appropriated by the notoriously plagiaristic Stillwell Company, which managed to have it included in the *Ladies Home Journal* bungalow book under the Stillwell name. (CSL.)

Mary Hill was the Woodworth client for 944 North Holliston Avenue, yet another early 1917 Kenneth Gordon design. This $5,000 Colonial Craftsman was a compactly planned one-and-a-half-story house with a full-width front porch. As seen here, there was also a cut-in porch at the rear, giving the living-room exterior views to both front and rear. (CSL.)

This alternative view of 944 North Holliston Avenue includes the garage and concrete driveway. All the Woodworth houses had single-car garages. By the mid-1910s, it was taken for granted that upper-middle-class families would own an automobile—but not two. After this house was started, the United States entered World War I in April 1917, and home building nearly stopped in Pasadena. (CSL.)

The bungalow at 1010 North Chester Avenue was constructed in the spring of 1919 when building picked up again following World War I. Tremendous inflation during the war caused prices and home costs almost to double, so this relatively small six-room English-style bungalow and garage cost $4,000. The corner living porch and driveway pergola reveal lingering Craftsman influences in this Kenneth Gordon design. (CSL.)

The bungalow at 1010 North Chester was sold to Henryette Ware (1884–1965), a young widow from Wisconsin who came to Pasadena via Chicago. Ware's household consisted of her daughter Ethel (later Ethel Sacks, 1906–1996) and her widowed mother, Ethel Berthelet (1855–1945). Ware remained at the house until her death in 1965. This 1924 view shows rapid landscape growth in five years. (CSL.)

A 1924 close-up of the front door of 1010 North Chester Avenue reveals an eyebrow roofline with curved gutter, an arched top edge of the door to go with the roof, two pairs of knee braces supporting a curved porch beam, and period planting pots. The corner porch, just visible on the left, was later enclosed. (CSL.)

This Woodworth-Gordon Colonial bungalow was built on the northeast corner of Chester Avenue and Mountain Street in mid-1919 for $4,500. Kenneth Gordon often used U-shaped plans; this house utilized a side-facing U layout, providing exceptional lighting and garden views in the rear rooms. Like 1010 North Chester, this design featured eyebrow curves in the porch and roof. (CSL.)

The bungalow at 1098 North Chester Avenue was constructed by the Woodworths on speculation in late 1919 for $5,000. This Kenneth Gordon design had a U-shaped plan and distinctive half-octagon entry porch. As in most of the other Gordon Colonials of this time frame, this one had decorative (non-functional) shutters and trellis accents. Note the horizontal lines created across the roof by double layers of shingles every fourth course or so. (CSL.)

Beginning in 1920, the Woodworths responded to the market demand for Spanish-style bungalows with a series of restrained Kenneth Gordon designs seeming to take their inspiration from the simple adobe ranch house. Among the first of these was 1168 North Chester Avenue, constructed in mid-1920 at a cost of $5,500. It was sold to George and Susan Pooley. (CSL.)

Another entry in the Woodworth-Gordon series of Spanish bungalows was built at 1159 North Chester Avenue in late 1920 for $5,500. The purchasers were dentist Gail Van Wye and his wife, Pearl. *U*-shaped plans like this shifted the focus of living to the rear, making the large front "living porch" obsolete. Gordon used this simple style in his own 1922 Altadena house, considered a classic. (CSL.)

Constructed at the same time as 1159 above, this $5,500 bungalow at 960 North Chester Avenue was yet another example of Gordon's simple version of the Spanish style. This one has a rectangular plan but features a private walled patio off the entry porch. In the background to the right is 965 North Holliston Avenue, a 1914 Woodworth Craftsman bungalow designed by D. M. Renton. (CSL.)

This street scene of North Chester Avenue, probably taken in the 1930s, shows street trees and landscaping that had achieved considerable growth since first planted. 1218 North Chester is on the left. The subdivisions north of the Woodworth Tract, including this section of Chester Avenue, were developed at the same time and seemed to follow the Woodworths' lead in lot sizes and building restrictions. (Courtesy of Karen Walter.)

The bungalow at 1218 North Chester Avenue is pictured here at the same time as the street scene above. It was built in 1922 for $5,000 by owner-builder-designer Henry Huffman, a local contractor. Light colors and symmetry add a hint of Colonial flavor to a late-Craftsman design. The 1920s saw a decrease in the use of over-scaled details and large timbers, resulting in a more refined appearance. (Courtesy of Karen Walter.)

Many English-style bungalows were constructed in Bungalow Heaven, especially on Chester and Holliston Avenues. This example was constructed at 1110 North Chester in early 1925 by contractor D.J. McKay of Los Angeles for Dennis Shannon at a cost of $5,500. The design was by Angelus Architectural Service, a Los Angeles firm in which draftsman Allen Bravender was a partner. (HL.)

Period revival styles continued to be built in and near the Woodworth Tract into the 1930s. This Spanish Colonial example at 950 North Holliston Avenue was constructed in 1926 for Ernest Bosca by La Dell Booth at a cost of $8,000; the view dates from 1946. Many vacant lots remained in this section until around World War II, when most were filled with simple 1940s stucco houses. (JAH-PMH Hawkins-1742.)

Six

COMMERCE
AND COMMUNITY

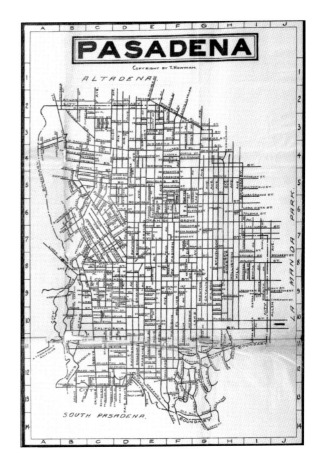

This 1912 map shows the Bungalow Heaven area after the 1906 East Pasadena annexation, the northeast Washington/Hill corner of the city grid. In the 1920s, Stevenson Avenue was renamed Mar Vista Avenue for the view of the Pacific Ocean from the top of the street. East of city limits is Lamanda Park, the name Sunny Slope vintner L.J. Rose and wife Amanda gave to their subdivision. (HL.)

A rainy North Lake Avenue, taken from Charles Francis Saunders's home, is shown before 1929 when the street was widened to ease automobile traffic. Opened in 1886, Lake Vineyard Avenue (later shortened) was named after Don Benito Wilson's ranch (see page 12) and was once a trail leading north from his property to Las Flores Canyon. Hoping to entice development, boosters named the northernmost segment Prospect Avenue, but the name was short-lived. (HL.)

North Lake Avenue, photographed here during the legendary snowstorm of January 1949, was once a quiet residential street but became one of Pasadena's major north-south arterials. Although it was still dotted with original bungalows, like the 1906 Charles Saunders home, after the 1929 widening some properties were subdivided and most homes removed, except between Bell and Claremont Streets, and replaced with businesses serving the surrounding neighborhoods. (JAH-PMH S39-41.)

In 1888, the Highland Railroad Company increased service from Colorado Street, with a horse-car line on North Lake Avenue from Villa Street to New York Avenue. Streetcar service was soon extended northward, taken over by the Pasadena and Los Angeles Electric Railway and by 1911 Henry Huntington's interurban Pacific Electric Red Car trolleys. The 2.32-mile North Lake Avenue Short Line was replaced with bus service in 1941. (PMH T12-44.)

Full-service rail transit operated until about 1925 in Pasadena, which became a commuter suburb of downtown Los Angeles. Interurban tourism grew, and Pasadena's population increased from 10,000 to 45,000 residents. While the backbone of streetcar service was along Colorado Street, secondary service began early on Lake Avenue, with more limited routes added later on East Villa Street, Orange Grove Boulevard, and Washington Boulevard, enabling growth in the northeast. (HL.)

To accommodate growth, the City of Pasadena's 1922 Zoning Map designated higher densities near North Lake Avenue and Washington Boulevard. Businesses would serve the growing community outside of the central district as well as tourists and nature enthusiasts on their way to the mountains. The northeast corner with its iconic and fondly remembered ice cream store was demolished after this 1946 photograph and is now a gas station. (JAH-PMH Hawkins-1636.)

By the Great Depression, the city had swelled to 76,000 inhabitants. Commerce had opened on both sides of Lake Avenue near Washington Boulevard, creating a walkable, neighborhood shopping district with continuous street frontage connected to public transit. The block on the southwest side, shown here in the 1950s, was eventually razed to make way for a parking lot and chain stores in an automobile-oriented shopping center. (JAH-PMH Hawkins-6017.)

This Harold A. Parker photograph from the late 1930s shows the Washington Hardware Store with its brick facade at 1403 North Lake Avenue. It was most likely built in 1930 by Arthur L. Fryer for R.M. Fulton. A Piggly Wiggly grocery store is next door to the left. A few buildings of similar style and materials remain along Lake Avenue north of Washington Boulevard. (HL.)

The Spanish Colonial Revival–style Washington Theater, designed by Clarence L. Jay near the Lake Avenue and Washington Boulevard intersection, was completed in 1924 after years of delays pending street paving. It was among the first multi-use projects, combining a Fox-operated, 900-seat movie palace with frontage shops, upstairs offices, and housing. Shown in its heyday, it became Cinema 21 in the 1970s but was closed indefinitely in 1989. (PMH T2-12.)

Henry W. Longfellow Elementary School, located at 1605 East Washington Boulevard, was originally designed in 1911 by Henry Mather Greene. The classical, reinforced concrete structure was to be the first "absolutely fireproof" school in the city. It was atypical of Greene and Greene "ultimate bungalows," the Gamble House, Blacker House, and other trendsetting Arts and Crafts–era residences he designed for wealthy clients with his brother Charles Sumner. (CSL.)

To serve a growing neighborhood, Longfellow Elementary School, at the edge of Bungalow Heaven on Washington Boulevard between Catalina and Mar Vista Avenues, underwent a number of alterations and additions in the 1920s and 1930s. Here, Greene's original Ionic pilasters and classical vocabulary are gone. The new Spanish Colonial Revival expansion designed by Sylvanus Marston added arches to the facade and a pitched roof. (HL.)

This photograph of Longfellow schoolchildren parading down Washington Boulevard for Halloween shows homes on the northern edge of Bungalow Heaven. To the left of the palm tree in the center is the Craftsman bungalow at the corner of Washington and Wilson Avenue that was demolished in the 1980s and replaced with a generic apartment building, launching neighborhood protest and preservation efforts. (FS-PMH 2-67-119.)

This 1920s view looking east from the center of Washington Boulevard from just west of Holliston Avenue shows the two-story 1914 Craftsman bungalow on the right, designed by D. M. Renton for the Schleicher family who had owned and subdivided the surrounding tract. The bungalow and the modest church building across the street remain. A larger chapel at the southeast corner was built on the vacant lot. (HL.)

At the center of Bungalow Heaven, on land the Cooley family once owned, McDonald Park was the second in Pasadena's neighborhood park system after Washington Park. Dedicated in 1920 to Judge Robert W. McDonald, who died in the 1918 influenza epidemic, its 1.23 acres contained a pergola and seating for 25 at the southern end of Pasadena Lake Vineyard Land and Water Company's Reservoir No. 3. (PMH P3-24.)

McDonald Park, intended for residents of the immediate area, had steep, grassy slopes and trees to screen the roofed-over Wilson Reservoir, abandoned in 1977. In the 1980s, the city developed the five-acre site, which included grading, landscaping, furniture, restrooms, ball courts, and a playing field. Local architect Russell Hobbs designed the Craftsman-style shade structure dedicated in 1997 as part of the neighborhood association's improvements. (PMH Vol. 58, p4.)

Seven

RESTORATION
AND RECOGNITION

Pasadena's early-20th-century beautification program included planting street trees, producing verdant canopies like this along Michigan Avenue. After World War II, larger ranch-style homes in automobile-oriented subdivisions farther from city centers were popular, and the 1972 Foothill Freeway extension split Pasadena in two. Both contributed to older, middle-class neighborhoods in the north becoming less sought after. Fortunately, most homes in Bungalow Heaven remained intact. (Photograph by James Staub.)

To comply with the Historic Preservation Act of 1976 and state mandates, Pasadena's Urban Conservation Office began surveying historic properties. During the process, John Merritt, a city planner (later the California Preservation Foundation's executive director) who lived on Michigan Avenue, coined the term "bungalow heaven" to describe the hundreds of small, older homes in the area; nonetheless, in 1985, this one was demolished. (Courtesy of City of Pasadena.)

The two-story 1912 Craftsman bungalow in the previous photograph was located at the corner of Wilson Avenue and Washington Boulevard on a lot zoned for multiple units. It was purchased for $82,000, bulldozed, and replaced with this uninspiring apartment building. Surrounding residents mobilized to prevent further demolitions, protect historic homes against incompatible remodeling, and address common neighborhood concerns, such as noise, crime, and traffic. (Photograph by James Staub.)

Neighborhood organizing resulted in reduction of residential densities, making new apartments uneconomical. To preserve single-family homes further, the Bungalow Heaven Neighborhood Association formed, with attorney Bill Crowfoot, a future city council member, as first president. On November 14, 1989, after preparing a Conservation Plan and conducting an eight-month petition drive showing 55 percent of property owners in support, the city council approved Pasadena's first landmark district. (Courtesy of Tina Miller.)

Pasadena graphic artist Toni Devereaux designed the official district street sign seen here. On April 10, 2008, twenty years after the city designated Bungalow Heaven its first local landmark district, acting upon the city's nomination and recommendation by the state, the US Department of Interior's National Park Service listed the Bungalow Heaven Historic District in the National Register of Historic Places. (Courtesy of Bungalow Heaven Neighborhood Association.)

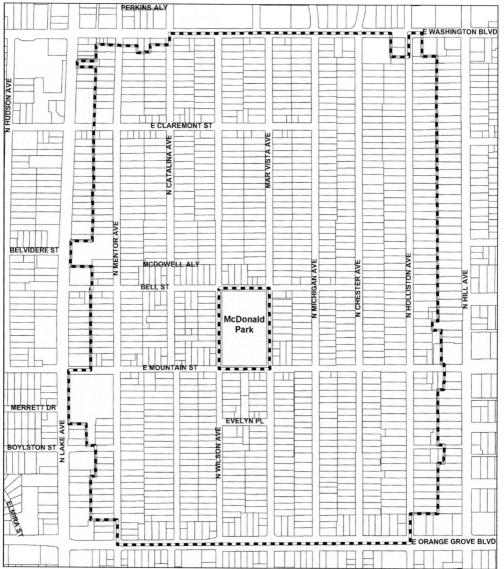

This official map shows the boundaries of the locally designated Bungalow Heaven Landmark District with McDonald Park at its center after Holliston Avenue was added in 2005. There are over 1,100 properties, none vacant, with a small number containing multiple units (mostly historic rear, second-unit cottages). In 1992, Nobel laureate Linus Pauling's modest home near the Caltech campus was moved to a lot on Mar Vista Avenue and restored, avoiding pending demolition. The neighborhood spans two city council districts (No. 2 and No. 5), resulting in political clout. It has a reputation for leadership and civic engagement, producing a mayor (Rick Cole), several city council members, and scores of commissioners. The private non-profit Bungalow Heaven Neighborhood Association, open to all residents and homeowners, strives "to preserve and improve the neighborhood . . . represent collective positions on issues . . . [and] provide a forum and vehicle for communication." To increase the number of structures contributing to landmark status, in 2003 the association launched a Home Restoration Grant Program to assist low- and moderate-income owners to make improvements. (Courtesy of City of Pasadena.)

On April 17, 1988, Pasadena Heritage, a citywide preservation group, held a Bungalow Heaven walking Home Tour, which the neighborhood association has continued to produce since 1990. The annual Home Tour attracts thousands who visit from six to eight properties, raising funds and neighborhood pride while celebrating admirable restoration efforts, such as those by planetary scientist Dr. Carol Polanskey, shown stripping paint from her bungalow. (Photograph by Kennon Miedema.)

This 1909 home at 1189 North Wilson Avenue, meticulously restored by owners Carol Polanskey and Martin Ratliff, was the first of 10 built by its original owner, contractor John K. Johnson. With its unusual combination of Victorian and Craftsman traits, it was featured on the 1996 and 2007 tours. Tour proceeds—used for revitalizing McDonald Park in the 1990s—pay for neighborhood gatherings and improvements. (Photograph by James Staub.)

Many stories of remarkable home restorations have contributed to revitalizing the neighborhood *Sunset Magazine* deemed in 2003 among the "West's Best." The 1885 folk Victorian Keil-Wilson house, the oldest structure, is shown a century later, a product of neglect in an era marked by demolitions, absentee landlordism, and citywide disregard for cultural resources before a grassroots historic preservation movement turned Pasadena around. (Courtesy of City of Pasadena.)

In the late 1990s, new owners bought the historic house, the only remaining example in Pasadena of the Gothic Revival style, and began restoring it. While efforts are still ongoing, the home Jennie Keil built at 714 North Mentor Avenue boasts a new foundation, restored front porch, repaired gingerbread and fish-scale siding, and appropriate new windows, among other features contributing to landmark status. (Photograph by James Staub.)

In 1911, Leora and Samuel Alvey, who ran a wallpaper business and lived next door, built this home at 939 North Michigan Avenue as a rental. Carl and Mary Ringhoff were the first owners to live in it full-time, from 1920 to 1960. Unfortunately, over the years, the front porch was enclosed to add interior space, period elements were lost, and obscuring fencing added. (Courtesy of City of Pasadena.)

Featured on the 1998 annual Home Tour, the bungalow was restored inside and out to its original Craftsman beauty by the current owner over the course of a year. Arroyo stone columns and an arched lintel now frame the opened-up front porch. The re-exposed east wall incorporates casement windows; the woodwork throughout was painstakingly stripped and refinished. (Photograph by James Staub.)

Designer-builders Hyde and Balch constructed four houses in the neighborhood, including 1272 North Catalina Avenue for Army captain Corwin Van Pelt and wife, Susie, for $2,200 in 1916. That year, the *Pasadena Star-News* illustrated its original appearance. Several owners and many renters later, arches were added to the front porch, and its clapboard siding and wooden window aprons lost, along with its Craftsman character. (Courtesy of City of Pasadena.)

On the 1999 annual Home Tour as a "restoration in progress," it is noticeable that the new owners have now dramatically returned the bungalow to its original Craftsman vocabulary by removing the Mediterranean arches to reveal the original wooden posts and brick piers, as well as removing the stucco and uncovering and restoring the original siding. On the interior, other efforts included stripping paint and opening up walled-in passageways. (Photograph by James Staub.)

This 1909 home at 1067 North Catalina Avenue was also on the 1999 tour but as the happy outcome of thoughtful restoration. Built for Arthur A. Jepson by the prolific contracting firm of Shilling and Luce that specialized in median-priced homes, by the 1960s the house had been "modernized," completely wrapped in aluminum siding that concealed the front dormer windows and other original features. (Courtesy of City of Pasadena.)

In the mid-1990s, owner Wayne Zitter, who restored at least four homes, rehabilitated this one. He removed the siding, repoured the front porch, constructed a pergola on the south side, added stairs to the second floor, rebuilt the kitchen and bathroom, and stripped and refinished the woodwork and Douglas-fir flooring throughout. The living room features built-ins and a handsome fireplace faced with iron-spot bricks. (Photograph by James Staub.)

This 1920 Spanish-style bungalow at 975 North Chester Avenue, modeled after the simple, adobe rancho houses of early California's colonial period, was built on speculation by real estate firm J.H. Woodworth and Son that had previously subdivided the 40-acre Tract no. 1945. Designed by Woodworth's architect Kenneth Gordon, it was first sold to Flora Uphof, a retired stenographer from Manhattan. (Courtesy of Leslie Tamppari.)

The current owners overhauled vegetation obscuring the front façade and reversed alterations out of character with the home's design. In replacing the lost bank of front windows and French doors, they carefully re-created them by copying the remaining original elements and repeating patterns consistent with other neighborhood houses designed by the same architect. The restored house was featured on the 2010 annual Home Tour. (Courtesy of Leslie Tamppari.)

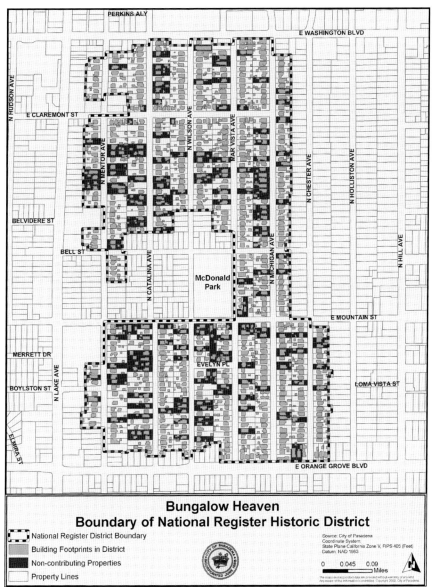

Bungalow Heaven
Boundary of National Register Historic District

National Register District Boundary

Building Footprints in District

Non-contributing Properties

Property Lines

Source: City of Pasadena
Coordinate System:
State Plane California Zone V, FIPS 405 (Feet)
Datum: NAD 1983

0   0.045   0.09
Miles

The maps and associated data are provided without warranty of any kind.
Any reuse of this information is prohibited. Copyright 2009, City of Pasadena.

The multiple-property Bungalow Heaven Historic District, listed in the National Register of Historic Places on April 10, 2008, has a period of significance of 1890 to 1929, reflecting the residential architecture in Pasadena of the Arts and Crafts movement. Few US neighborhoods remain with the same high level of physical integrity. This map shows 684 parcels within irregular yet contiguous boundaries, with 521 contributing and 165 non-contributing structures (686 buildings). Not included are McDonald Park, originally a reservoir, and homes on the eastern end of the landmark district that tend to be larger and later (1920s–1940s). The oldest homes are generally on the southwest, the neighborhood having grown from Lake Avenue eastward. Michigan Avenue (called Ellis Avenue before about 1910) has the most continuous concentration of Craftsman bungalows. In 2009, partly because of its human scale and outstanding architecture, the American Planning Association named Bungalow Heaven a "Great Neighborhood" in its Great Places in America program. The saying goes that people "come for the houses and stay for the neighborhood." (Courtesy of City of Pasadena.)

DISCOVER THOUSANDS OF LOCAL HISTORY BOOKS FEATURING MILLIONS OF VINTAGE IMAGES

Arcadia Publishing, the leading local history publisher in the United States, is committed to making history accessible and meaningful through publishing books that celebrate and preserve the heritage of America's people and places.

Find more books like this at
www.arcadiapublishing.com

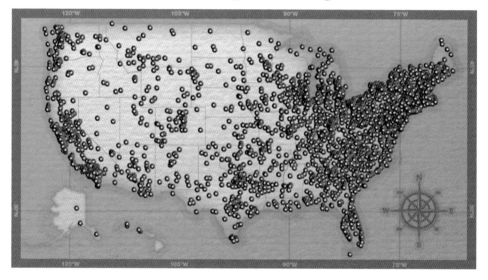

Search for your hometown history, your old
stomping grounds, and even your favorite sports team.